Literary Britain and Ireland

A GUIDE TO THE PLACES THAT INSPIRED POETS, PLAYWRIGHTS AND NOVELISTS

**JANE STRUTHERS
AND CHRIS COE**

First published in 2005 by New Holland Publishers (UK) Ltd
London • Cape Town • Sydney • Auckland

www.newhollandpublishers.com

Garfield House, 86–88 Edgware Road, London W2 2EA, United Kingdom

80 McKenzie Street, Cape Town 8001, South Africa

14 Aquatic Drive, Frenchs Forest, NSW 2086, Australia

218 Lake Road, Northcote, Auckland, New Zealand

10 9 8 7 6 5 4 3 2 1

ISBN 1 84330 901 7

Publishing Manager: Jo Hemmings
Senior Editor: Kate Michell
Assistant Editor: Kate Parker
Cover Design and Design: Alan Marshall
Cartography: Bill Smuts
Indexer: Dorothy Frame
Production: Joan Woodroffe

Reproduction by Pica Digital Pte Ltd, Singapore
Printed and bound in Singapore by Kyodo Printing Co. (Singapore) Pte Ltd

Photographs appearing on the cover, prelim pages and page 160 are as
follows:
Front cover (main picture): Agatha Christie's desk, Torre Abbey, Torquay,
Devon; (portraits left to right): William Shakespeare, Virginia Woolf,
Oscar Wilde, Charlotte Brontë, Lord Byron, Dylan Thomas.
Back cover, clockwise from top left: St Margaret's Bay, Dover, Kent;
Thomas Hardy's Cottage, Higher Bockhampton, Dorset; Bateman's,
Burwash, East Sussex; Shandy Hall, Coxwold, North Yorkshire.
Front cover flap: Trinity College, Dublin, Eire.
Page 1: First editions on display at Eton College Library, Windsor, Berkshire.
Opposite: Carlyle's House, Chelsea, London.
Pages 4–5: Llyn Peninsula, Gwynedd, Wales.
Page 160: Plas Newydd, Llangollen, Denbighshire, Wales.

Dedication
To my mother, Jean, and in memory of my grandfather, Len – who both
encouraged me to believe that few things are more important than being
absorbed in a good book.

Contents

Introduction

Reading a book is one of the great joys in life. It can be – and often is – addictive. It involves entering the world of an author's imagination and spending time with them while they recount their tale to us. It's no wonder that our favourite authors can start to feel like old friends, because we take so much pleasure from being in their company. We may never meet them, but we feel we know them in some essential way, because we have heard their voices, been touched by their emotions and viewed life from their perspective. This is true whether the writer in question is a poet, playwright, novelist, critic or essayist.

All great writers create their own universe, often with a basis in reality, whether it is Graham Greene's 'Greeneland', Thomas Hardy's Wessex, Daphne du Maurier's Cornwall or Evelyn Waugh's Oxford, and although the writing takes us to these places in our minds it is fascinating to actually visit them. There is nothing new about this. When Alfred, Lord Tennyson visited Lyme Regis in Dorset the first thing he wanted to do was to see the Cobb where Louisa Musgrove fell down in Jane Austen's *Persuasion*.

Literary Britain and Ireland is, therefore, a guide to many of the places associated with writers. Wherever possible, I have chosen places that are open to the public, whether they are the houses that the authors lived in or the graveyards where they are buried. There are also museums dedicated to their memories, statues that celebrate their lives and landscapes that inspired them. The book is arranged geographically into ten

BELOW: The Red House in Bexleyheath, just outside London, was the home of novelist and Arts and Crafts pioneer William Morris.

BELOW: In Laugharne, Dylan Thomas had a worskhed just above his home, The Boathouse, overlooking the estuary.

regions, covering England, Scotland, Wales and both Northern Ireland and Eire, with maps to show where the places can be found so you can visit them yourself.

Of course, these places are a personal selection because it would be impossible to cram every house, church, town, village and landscape in Britain and Ireland with a literary connection into a single illustrated work. In choosing the places that appear in this book, I have looked for those that are irrevocably associated with a particular author, such as Hill Top Farm, where Beatrix Potter once lived, and those that have the strongest or most interesting links, such as Howth Head where Erskine Childers rowed ashore with a cargo of illegal guns.

The most celebrated English, Welsh, Scottish and Irish writers are included, among them Virginia Woolf, Dylan Thomas, Sir Walter Scott and W.B. Yeats. But there are many lesser-known names besides, and the book covers a wide range of genres, including travel writing, comic novels, light fiction, pot-boilers, crime novels, gothic chillers, serious poems, humorous verse, children's novels, autobiographies, biographies, memoirs and stream of consciousness fiction.

As well as getting enjoyment from reading the book itself, and visiting the places it mentions, I hope that your interest will be awakened in those authors you have never read before so the book introduces you to some new friends as well as reuniting you with old ones.

Jane Struthers

BELOW: The county town of Lincoln commemorates local boy and poet laureate Alfred, Lord Tennyson with a prominent statue.

BELOW: Knole in Sevenoaks, Kent, was the childhood home of novelist Vita Sackville-West.

CHAPTER 1

South-west England

AGATHA CHRISTIE

From the elegant Regency crescents of Bath to the rugged coastline of Cornwall, from the wilds of Dartmoor to the palm trees of Torquay, the south-west of England offers a rich variety of moods and landscapes. It has inspired many great writers, some of whom have created their own worlds within these counties. Thomas Hardy, while living and writing in his native Dorset, conjured up the mythical county of Wessex in which many of his novels were set. Daphne du Maurier's imagination and heart were similarly captured by Cornwall, prompting her to write a succession of period romances and novels that were inspired by the countryside and houses around Fowey. The magic of the West Country continues to captivate contemporary writers, including John Fowles who has written about Lyme Regis, where he lives, and Sean O'Casey, who spent many years living in Devon.

T.E. LAWRENCE

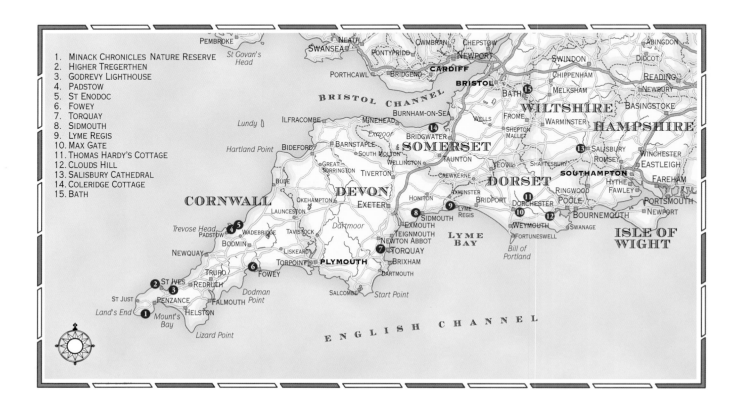

1. MINACK CHRONICLES NATURE RESERVE
2. HIGHER TREGERTHEN
3. GODREVY LIGHTHOUSE
4. PADSTOW
5. ST ENODOC
6. FOWEY
7. TORQUAY
8. SIDMOUTH
9. LYME REGIS
10. MAX GATE
11. THOMAS HARDY'S COTTAGE
12. CLOUDS HILL
13. SALISBURY CATHEDRAL
14. COLERIDGE COTTAGE
15. BATH

Minack Chronicles Nature Reserve

DORMINACK, CORNWALL

In 1950, Derek (1912–96) and Jeannie Tangye (1919–86) decided that their life in London was over. Derek was a Fleet Street journalist and author, and Jeannie was the public relations officer for the Savoy Hotel. It had been fun living in London, but its charms had now palled and they were ready for a new challenge. They certainly found it.

They moved to Dorminack in Cornwall, which was a flower farm and cottage that had definitely seen

better days. Living there was very hard work, but they loved it and were surrounded by animals. In 1961, Derek wrote the first of 20 books about life at the farm, which not only detailed the concerns of its human inhabitants, but those of the Tangyes' beloved donkeys and cats as well. The books, which Jeannie illustrated, quickly became popular for their gentle charm and their evocation of rural life, and readers sometimes visited the farm so they could meet the animals and people that they enjoyed reading about so much. Many of these experiences, which were not always as pleasant as one might hope, went into what became known as the Minack Chronicles. A donkey named Oliver was a particular star of the books and gained a strong human following that could sometimes be a nuisance.

In 1979, Oliver gave his name to the 20-acre stretch of wild coastline adjoining the Tangyes' farm. They bought the land and called it Oliver Land, and it became the Minack Chronicles Nature Reserve. It was open to the public, although it was emphasized that it was a place for solitude and contemplation.

Jeannie died in 1986; her illness and death were poignantly recorded in the books, and Derek died at Minack ten years later. His ashes were scattered in the Honeysuckle Meadow of the Nature Reserve on 23 March, which is known to Minack followers as Jeannie's Memorial Day because it was her birthday. After her death, Derek asked that every Minack devotee should spend a few minutes in silent contemplation on each Memorial Day because they would then be at Minack in spirit.

Higher Tregerthen

NEAR ZENNOR, CORNWALL

Late in 1915, D.H. Lawrence (1885– 1930) and his wife, Frieda, decided to leave London and move to Cornwall,

LEFT: The sanctuary created by Derek and Jeannie Tangye for humans and animals alike lives on in the Minack Chronicles Nature Reserve at Dorminack.

PREVIOUS PAGE: Agatha Christie typed many of her books on this 1937 Remington typewriter which is part of an exhibition dedicated to the detective fiction writer at Torre Abbey in Torquay.

which they hoped would be a much more congenial place to live. They thought that the move might also improve Lawrence's health, which was so bad that it had forced him to give up his teaching career. Above all, Lawrence and Frieda dreamed of creating a small but select literary community with the New Zealand-born novelist Katherine Mansfield (1888–1923), and her lover and later husband, John Middleton Murry (1889–1957), who was then editor of the modernist periodical *Rhythm*. The two couples had become friends, although it was rather a volatile connection, peppered with outbursts and heavy with artistic temperament.

At the time, Lawrence was still smarting from the furore that had surrounded the publication of his novel *The Rainbow* (1915) and its subsequent suppression for obscenity. It cannot have helped that his publisher, Methuen, said they 'regretted having published it', nor that his literary friends were against the idea of censorship in general but refused to champion this book in particular. Retreat to Cornwall seemed to be the best option, even though the period turned out to be fraught with difficulties, as did so much of Lawrence's life.

ABOVE: D.H. Lawrence and his wife, Frieda, stayed at the Tinker's Arms in Zennor in the spring of 1916 while searching for a cottage to rent. Their 18-month stay in Cornwall was not a success.

In March 1916, the Lawrences found two adjoining cottages available for rent in Higher Tregerthen, a short distance from Zennor. These seemed ideal, as the Lawrences could live in one and Katherine and John could have the other one. Mansfield and Murry arrived in April and the experiment was initially a success. However, the atmosphere quickly soured and the foursome became disgruntled: Katherine was depressed by the sound of seagulls; Murry felt threatened by the sexual overtures that Lawrence was making to him; Frieda felt unable to join in the others' literary conversations and Lawrence found Murry's company difficult. After two months Katherine and Murry moved out.

Although the literary commune had come to nothing, it gave Lawrence valuable inspiration for the novel he had begun to work on in April 1916 – *Women in Love*, which was published in 1921. He and Frieda were cast as Birkin and Ursula, and Katherine and

ABOVE: Godrevy Lighthouse inspired Virginia Woolf to write *To The Lighthouse*; it also featured in Rosamunde Pilcher's novel *The Shell Seekers* (1987), which was set in St Ives.

to throw themselves on the mercy of a succession of friends until they found a cottage in Middleton-by-Wirksworth in the Midlands. Two years later the Lawrences had had enough of England and moved to Italy. Lawrence never felt the same about his homeland again.

Godrevy Lighthouse

GWITHIAN, CORNWALL

Each summer the Stephen family spent their holidays at Talland House, near St Ives. Sir Leslie Stephen (1832–1904) bought the house in 1882, the same year that his youngest child, Virginia (1882–1941), was born. The house was always full of people, including a young boy called Rupert Brooke (1887–1915), who went on to become a celebrated poet (see pages 65–6). The happy memories of summers spent paddling, fishing, sailing and swimming soaked into Virginia's mind and later emerged in several of the novels she wrote under her married name of Woolf – *Jacob's Room* (1922) *The Waves* (1931) and, most notably, *To The Lighthouse* (1927). The Stephen family continued to visit St Ives until just before the death of Virginia's mother, Julia, in 1895. The four Stephen children – Vanessa, Thoby, Adrian and Virginia – revisited St Ives and Talland House in the summer of 1905, following the death of their father the year before.

To The Lighthouse drew on Virginia's memories of the Cornish countryside around Godrevy Lighthouse, which stands close to the bay of St Ives and is visible for miles around. Although she set the book in the Hebrides, it is full of her feelings for Cornwall. The first part of the novel also drew heavily on Virginia's memories of her mother and father, who appear as the gracious Mrs Ramsey and the emotionally demanding Mr Ramsey.

Murry as Gudrun and Gerald. When they read it, the Murrys were not pleased. Neither was the literary hostess Lady Ottoline Morrell (1873–1938), who was given a copy of the manuscript by chance before the book was published. She immediately recognized herself as the eccentric character of Hermione and was hugely offended by the portrait. It was the end of her friendship with Lawrence, who was never invited to her home at Garsington Manor (see page 79) again.

The Lawrences lived at Higher Tregerthen until October 1917 when, following police surveillance and the growing suspicion of the locals that they were German spies, the cottage was raided by the police and some of Lawrence's manuscripts were taken away for examination. It was the end of the Cornish idyll, and the couple returned to London where they were forced

Padstow

CORNWALL

North Cornwall was the spiritual home of the poet Sir John Betjeman (1906–84). As far as he was concerned, there was 'splendour, splendour everywhere' throughout the county, which he had loved since he first visited Daymer Bay as a boy. He chronicled his love of Cornwall in both poetry and prose, including such disparate works as *The Shell*

Guide to Cornwall (1934) and *Summoned by Bells* (1960). The latter, an autobiography in blank-verse that spans the period from his childhood until he went to university at Oxford, described Betjeman's enjoyment of his Cornish holidays.

Betjeman described his personal experience of Cornwall, of coming home on the Padstow ferry 'on a fine, still evening, laden with the week's shopping', and his particular love of the stretch of railway from Wadebridge to Padstow. His book, *Cornwall* (1964), is an idiosyncratic guide to the place he knew, taking the reader across beaches, into coves and around tiny churches. His love of the county is remembered in the Betjeman Centre, which is situated at the old railway station in Wadebridge and has information about Betjeman's connections with the area.

Betjeman was not the first poet to have discovered the delights of Padstow and its surrounding countryside. The Elizabethan courtier and poet Sir Walter Ralegh (*c.* 1554–1618) was Warden of Cornwall from 1585 and stayed at Ralegh's Court House on South Quay in Padstow when he was in the county.

St Enodoc

ROCK, CORNWALL

As Poet Laureate, Sir John Betjeman could have opted for a grand burial in Westminster Abbey when he died from Parkinson's Disease in 1984, but instead he made it clear that he wanted to be buried in the churchyard at St Enodoc in Rock. It was a characteristic decision by a man who spent a great deal of his professional life writing about England's churches, villages and architecture, and who was devoted to Cornwall. He had first come to the county as a schoolboy on his summer holidays, when he and his parents stayed in Trebetherick near Padstow (see page 12). Betjeman had a particular love of old churches and took great pleasure in exploring those in Cornwall.

St Juliot, another interesting church with literary connections, lies a few miles to the north-east of St Enodoc. In 1870, the Revd Gifford, rector of St Juliot, realized that his 13th-century church needed some restoration, and a young architect called Thomas Hardy (1840–1928) arrived to give his considered opinion. When he called at the rectory (now a private house), he met the rector's sister, Emma, and fell in love with her. Thomas and Emma were married in 1874 and spent their honeymoon in Brighton. In memory of this, St Juliot appears as St Agnes in *A Pair of Blue Eyes* (1873).

In quest of mystical experience I knelt in darkness at St Enodoc

SIR JOHN BETJEMAN, *SUMMONED BY BELLS*

Fowey

CORNWALL

For Kenneth Grahame (1859–1932), the delights of the Cornish fishing village of Fowey and the chance to 'mess about in boats' formed the perfect contrast to his work in the City of London. He first visited the town in 1899, a year after he became

BELOW: Padstow was greatly loved by Sir John Betjeman, but D.H. Lawrence, who spent the winter of 1915 here, was not happy about the way the wind whipped the sea into spray.

Secretary of the Bank of England, and he was entranced by the place. So much so, that he married Elspeth Thomson in Fowey that July, at St Fimbarrus' Church, with his great friend, Sir Arthur Quiller-Couch (1863–1944) in attendance. After a short honeymoon, Grahame and his wife returned to Fowey where he was able to continue the joys of boating with Quiller-Couch. It seems that there were far more joys to be had with his friend than with Elspeth, whose snobbish attitudes grated on her husband. It was not a happy marriage.

At the time, Quiller-Couch, popularly known as 'Q', was putting the finishing touches to the first edition of *The Oxford Book of English Verse* (1900), which he was editing. He lived and worked in The Haven, on the Esplanade in Fowey, from 1892 until his death in 1944. Q was a prolific writer whose first adventure story, *Dead Man's Rock*, was published in 1887. A year later he wrote *The Astonishing History of Troy Town*, the Troy Town of the title being Fowey by another name. It was the first of several novels about the town, whose occupants were sufficiently pleased to elect Quiller-Couch mayor in 1937.

In 1907, Kenneth and Elspeth Grahame returned to Cornwall for a short holiday while their only child, Alastair, stayed in Sussex with his governess. Grahame, who was already a published author, began to write letters to his son that formed the beginnings of what became *The Wind in the Willows* (1908). Initially the book received a lukewarm reception, but it eventually became a children's classic. Grahame retired from the Bank of England in 1907, which enabled him to continue to write and to enjoy the pleasures of Fowey as well as the company of Q and his family.

In 1926 the du Maurier family bought a holiday house, Ferryside, next to the Bodinnick ferry. The young Daphne du Maurier (1907–89) often stayed on in Cornwall after the rest of her family had returned to London each year, and busied herself exploring the coastline both on foot and by boat. She was also busy writing, and her first novel, *The Loving Spirit*, was published to great acclaim in 1931. By this time she was great friends with the Quiller-Couch family and often went riding with their daughter, Foy, over Bodmin Moor.

The Loving Spirit made such an impact on a certain Major Tommy 'Boy' Browning that he sailed into

BELOW: The little church of St Enodoc, where Sir John Betjeman is buried, appeared in Sabine Baring-Gould's novel about Cornish wreckers, *In the Roar of the Sea* (1892).

Fowey harbour to meet its author. The result of this meeting could have come straight from one of Daphne's novels – they fell in love and were married in July 1932 at St Wyllow's Church, Lanteglos.

Daphne had fallen deeply in love once before when, in 1927, she stumbled across the house that obsessed her for the rest of her life. This was Menabilly, which she turned into Manderley in her celebrated gothic thriller-romance, *Rebecca* (1938). She finally managed to live there in 1943, but only as a tenant because the owners – the Rashleigh family – refused to sell it to her. The house was also the setting for *The King's General* (1946) and *My Cousin Rachel* (1951).

The inevitable happened in 1967, when the lease on Menabilly ran out and Daphne was forced to leave. She moved to Kilmarth, above Polkerris, which she immortalized in *The House on the Strand* (1969), but she still yearned for Menabilly. She wrote about her love for her adoptive county in almost all her books, and died in Par in April 1989.

Torquay

DEVON

In August 1838, the poet Elizabeth Barrett (1806–61) was sent to the Devon resort of Torquay for the sake of her health, having spent time in nearby Sidmouth some years before (see page 17).

ABOVE: The seaside town of Fowey has worked its charms on many writers, including Sir Arthur Quiller-Couch (who wrote about it as Troy Town), Kenneth Grahame and Daphne du Maurier.

Always frail, and with an over-protective father who was attuned to the slightest change in her condition, Elizabeth was fully accustomed to the life of an invalid. In fact, she was outraged that her Torquay doctor made her get up at ten in the morning instead of at noon, as was her habit in London. But the worst aspect of the convalescence was that the doctor forbade her to write, despite the fact that Elizabeth had published a volume of verse, *The Seraphim, and Other Poems*, to critical acclaim in June of that year.

Elizabeth settled at 1 Beacon Terrace, where the Hotel Regina now stands, along with her favourite brother, Edward, whom she called 'Bro'. The company of her adored Bro helped to mitigate her frustration at being confined to Torquay when she longed to be back in London where she could pursue her literary career.

In February 1840, another of Elizabeth's brothers, Sam, died of fever in Jamaica, but worse was to come. In July, Bro drowned in a boating accident east of Teignmouth. He had gone out with three friends and failed to return. No one knew what had happened to him until three weeks later when his body was washed up in Babbacombe Bay. Elizabeth's grief prevented her from writing anything for months, and gave her a hatred of the sight and sound of the sea. She was finally allowed

as she was not allowed to attend school. However, the young Agatha remedied this situation by teaching herself to read at the age of five. Her childhood at Ashfield made a tremendous impression on her; in *An Autobiography* (1977) she wrote 'I dream a great deal and always about Ashfield.'

Agatha was baptized at All Saints Church, Bampfylde Road when she was two months old, and her religious faith remained important to her throughout her life. The church had recently been rebuilt, partly through the generosity of Agatha's father who ensured that his infant daughter was listed as a founder member of the church.

to return to London in September 1841, her stay in Torquay being one of the worst experiences of her life.

The writer who is perhaps most associated with Torquay is Agatha Christie (1890–1976), who wrote over 70 detective novels set in a respectable, upper-middle-class world of teashops, maids, ruthless spinsters and ageing colonels. She was born Agatha Miller in the town and grew up in Ashfield, the family house in Barton Road, where she was educated by governesses,

ABOVE & BELOW: Agatha Christie is known worldwide as one of the great crime novelists of the 20th century. She was born and grew up in Torquay, and a special room at Torre Abbey in the town has been set aside in her memory; it contains many of her books and photographs.

As a teenager, she gained invaluable experience for her later profession as a crime writer by working as a Saturday girl in a pharmacy in Trematon Avenue, where she learned a great deal about poisons – poisoning was a method particularly favoured by her characters. She later trained as a pharmacist and worked in the dispensary at Torre Hospital during both world wars. Torre also provided important information on ecclesiastical matters for Christie's novels as she telephoned the parish vicar whenever she needed such information.

Like all writers, Agatha drew heavily on her own life and experiences for her books, and many places in Torquay were reproduced in her novels. She regularly took the steam train from Paignton to Churston, and

her Belgian detective, Hercule Poirot, travelled on this line in *The ABC Murders* (1936) and *Dead Man's Folly* (1956). Christie, in turn, is remembered in many different sites throughout Torquay, and a special room is devoted to her memory at Torre Abbey. She lived in Torquay until 1938, but later owned Greenway, in Galmpton near Brixham, the garden of which is now open to the public through the National Trust.

Another literary character associated with Torquay is the Irish playwright, Sean O'Casey

(1880–1964), who moved with his wife, Eileen, from nearby Totnes to the suburb of St Marychurch in Torquay in 1954 and lived here until his death ten years later.

Sidmouth

DEVON

The precarious health of the young poet, Miss Elizabeth Barrett, was a torment to her widowed father, Edward, for years. She suffered from a weak chest, which may have been caused by tuberculosis, and she also showed signs of what is now understood to be anorexia nervosa. Another torment to Edward Barrett was his financial state, which led to the sale of the family house in Hope End, Ledbury, Hertfordshire, in August 1832 when Elizabeth was 26. The family decamped to Sidmouth in Devon, an elegant seaside town that was considered beneficial for Elizabeth's health. At first they stayed at 7–8 Fortfield

BELOW: Elizabeth Barrett came to Sidmouth in 1832, in the hope that the balmy air would improve her health. She became friendly with the Reverend George Hunter, whose love for her was not reciprocated.

Terrace, moving to Belle Vue (now the Cedar Shade Hotel) in All Saints Road the following year.

Although most of the large Barrett family enjoyed life at the seaside, Elizabeth felt starved of intellectual company. She compensated for this by working at a translation from the Greek of *Prometheus Bound* by Aeschylus, as well as 19 poems, which were published in May 1833. In the autumn of 1835 the family moved to Wimpole Street, London (see page 51), a move that also saw the return of Elizabeth's ill-health.

Lyme Regis

DORSET

In the summer of 1804, the Austen family stayed at the seaside town of Lyme Regis, which had recently become fashionable. It was their second visit to the town. Among the party was Jane (1775–1817), who was 29 and trying hard to become a published writer. She was unmarried and living with her parents in Bath (see page 23).

Jane was a prolific letter-writer, particularly to her sister, Cassandra (1773–1845), who left Lyme Regis that September to stay with their brother, Henry, and

his wife, Eliza, in Weymouth. In a letter to Cassandra, Jane described her experiences in Lyme Regis, including dancing in the Assembly Rooms and wearing herself out by bathing in the sea. She also walked along the Cobb, which is the stone jetty that projects out to sea from the shore.

Jane's holiday in Lyme Regis became food for one of the most important scenes in her later novel, *Persuasion* (1818), which she began writing in 1815. In it, Louisa Musgrove has to be 'jumped down' the steps of the Cobb by Captain Wentworth, but she falls and is 'taken up lifeless'. This event carries such dramatic power that years later when Alfred, Lord Tennyson (1809–92) visited Lyme Regis he insisted on being taken straight to the Cobb, demanding, 'Show me the steps from which Louisa Musgrove fell!'

The Cobb was later immortalized in print once again, this time by John Fowles (born 1926) in the novel *The French Lieutenant's Woman* (1969). His heroine, the mysterious Sarah Woodruff, has a habit of standing on the Cobb staring out to sea.

Max Gate

DORCHESTER, DORSET

Thomas Hardy knew Dorchester all his life, having gone to school here. He grew up in nearby Higher Bockhampton (see below), but left in 1874 to live in London with his first wife, Emma. However, after trying out various homes, which were all unsatisfactory for one reason or the other, the Hardys finally settled back in Dorchester.

Hardy was trained as an architect, so he naturally wanted to design his new home. Work began on the house in November 1883, and the Hardys spent their first night here in June 1885. Although Hardy described Max Gate as 'only a cottage in the country which I use for writing in', it was much more imposing than that and proclaimed loudly that Hardy had graduated from his humble beginnings to an enviable prosperity. Nevertheless, Hardy spent a good part of each year in London or abroad, and Max Gate felt 'lonely and cottage-like' to him. It did not help that the Hardy's marriage was largely unhappy and emotionally chilly, although Hardy looked back on it with romantic nostalgia in the love poems he wrote after Emma's death in 1912.

Hardy wrote his later novels while cloistered in his study at Max Gate – *The Woodlanders* (1887), *Tess of the D'Urbervilles* (1891), *The Well-Beloved* (1892) and his final novel, *Jude the Obscure* (1896). Hardy had long chafed under the criticisms of reviewers who complained of the immoral and pessimistic nature of his novels, but the fuss over the publication of *Jude the Obscure*, which involved adult seduction and child suicide, was so great that he felt compelled to stop writing novels altogether. He concentrated on poetry instead, which he had always loved.

After Emma's death – some of his verse suggested that her ghost haunted Max Gate – Hardy married Florence Dugdale in 1914. Although immersed in his poetry, he also had a busy social life, entertaining the literary lions of the day, including the poet Siegfried Sassoon (1886–1967), T.E. Lawrence – who lived nearby at Clouds Hill (see pages 19–20) – J.M. Barrie (1860–1937), W.B. Yeats (1865–1939) and Virginia Woolf.

Hardy died at Max Gate in January 1928. Just as in life he had divided his time between Dorset and London, so in death he did the same: his heart was buried near the family graves in Stinsford church and his ashes were interred in Westminster Abbey (see pages 53–4). This arrangement went against Hardy's personal wish to be buried in Stinsford, but he was such a literary giant by the time of his death that it was generally felt that the abbey was the most fitting place for him. The Poet Laureate Cecil Day-Lewis (1904–72), who was a tremendous fan of Hardy, was buried in Stinsford churchyard in 1972.

Thomas Hardy's Cottage

HIGHER BOCKHAMPTON, DORSET

This tiny rural dwelling is where Thomas Hardy was born and spent the first 24 years of his life. Even today the cottage can only be reached by a ten-minute walk through the woods, and when the

OPPOSITE: Jane Austen first visited Lyme Regis in 1803. The town had recently become fashionable, helped by the Napoleonic Wars which made foreign travel inadvisable.

ABOVE: Hardy's Cottage, where Thomas Hardy was born and grew up, has a picturesque setting that he described in loving detail in his earliest-known poem, 'Domicilium'.

young Thomas Hardy was growing up here he had to tramp six miles to school in Dorchester each morning, and then do the return journey in the evening. The experience encouraged an acute awareness of his surroundings, and his novels are notable for their vivid descriptions of the Dorset countryside.

In his second published novel, *Under the Greenwood Tree* (1872), the cottage appears as Tranter Dewy's house, and Hardy wrote the book in his bedroom there. *Far from the Madding Crowd* (1874) was also written at the cottage, and when the weather was fine Hardy wrote in the garden. However, there were drawbacks to this as he sometimes ran out of paper at the point where inspiration was beginning to flow, and, rather than risk breaking his train of thought by going indoors, he wrote on whatever came to hand, whether it was an old leaf or a piece of slate.

By the time *Far from the Madding Crowd* was published, Hardy had moved out of the cottage and was living in less rural surroundings in Surbiton, Surrey with his wife, Emma. Although for a time he oscillated between London and Dorset, he finally moved to Max Gate (see page 18) in his home county not only for health reasons, but because he wanted to stay close

to his family. Besides, his writing was so steeped in Dorset and its neighbouring counties – which he called Wessex in his novels – that he needed to live in the region to gain the greatest inspiration from it.

Clouds Hill

WAREHAM, DORSET

When T. E. Lawrence (1888–1935) first rented Clouds Hill in 1923, he was retreating not only from the fame that he had garnered during the First World War as 'Lawrence of Arabia', but also from the infelicities of army life at nearby Bovington Camp, where he was known as T. E. Shaw of the Tank Corps. Lawrence had already gone through one name change, having enlisted in the RAF (to which he later returned) the year before as John Hume Ross. He loved Clouds Hill and commented that it reminded him of Egdon Heath in Thomas Hardy's novel *The Return of the Native* (1878). Lawrence was right about the effect of the countryside on Hardy as he was a near neighbour and friend (see pages 18–19).

ABOVE: The tiny, whitewashed Clouds Hill was home to T.E. Lawrence during the last years of his life. At first he used it as an evening retreat from life in the Army, but he later lived here permanently.

In 1924, Lawrence wrote of Clouds Hill to a friend: 'I don't sleep here, but come… nearly every evening, & dream, or write or read by the fire.' His writing involved revising the manuscript of *The Seven Pillars of Wisdom*, his account of the Arab Revolt, for which he received tremendous encouragement from his friends E.M. Forster, Thomas Hardy and George Bernard Shaw. The book was published in a limited, private edition in 1926 and was not published for the wider market until 1935.

Lawrence was discharged from the RAF in February 1935 and looked forward to a more relaxed life at Clouds Hill, which he had bought by this time. One of his greatest pleasures in life was riding motorcycles and he owned several over the years. He named them all Boanerges, after the sons of thunder in the Bible, and loved roaring along the Dorset lanes on whichever 'wild beast' he happened to own at the time.

Lawrence had survived the dangers of desert life during the First World War but he was killed by his passion for motorcycles. In the middle of May 1935, he rode into his local village to send a telegram to Henry Williamson (1895–1977), the author of *Tarka the Otter* (1927), and swerved on the way home to avoid two schoolboys. He was thrown headfirst into the road and died several days later. Lawrence was buried in the churchyard of St Nicholas's Church, Moreton. There is also a memorial to him at St Michael's Church, Wareham: it is a stone effigy of him in Arab costume, which was sculpted by his friend, Eric Kennington (1888–1960).

Salisbury Cathedral

SALISBURY, WILTSHIRE

On 10 June 1668, Samuel Pepys recorded in his diary that he thought Salisbury was 'greater than Oxford'. However, he was less impressed with his lodgings – 'the reckoning was so exorbitant' – which were at the George Inn. This 14th-century coaching inn has now vanished except for its gables, which can still be seen above the entrance to the Old George Mall. Pepys also visited Stonehenge, which he found most impressive despite being puzzled about why it had ever been built.

For Anthony Trollope (1815–82), an evening stroll around Salisbury Cathedral provided the idea for his novel *The Warden* (1855) which was set in the cathedral town of Barchester. His fictional town also borrowed heavily on nearby Winchester (see page 26).

For Thomas Hardy, many years later, Salisbury became Melchester in his sequence of Wessex novels. It features particularly strongly in *Jude the Obscure* (1896), and is where Jude's cousin and great love, Sue Bridehead, goes to college. The relationship ends in tragedy, and the novel was considered

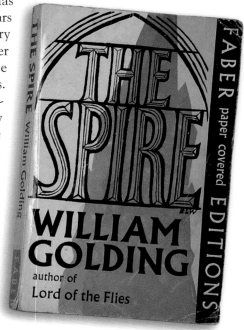

to be so depressing and immoral that Hardy never wrote another novel.

Charles Dickens also made great use of Salisbury in *Martin Chuzzlewit* (1844), as the home of the egregious widower and hypocrite, Mr Pecksniff. When Tom Pinch, who is Mr Pecksniff's assistant, arrives in Salisbury he 'set forth on a stroll about the streets with a vague and not unpleasant idea that they teemed with all kinds of mystery and bedevilment'. However, most of the bedevilment in his life came from his employer.

As far as the novelist E.M. Forster (1879–1970) was concerned, Salisbury Cathedral had 'the most beautiful spire in the world'. Forster was familiar with the city because he used to stay here with friends who lived at 13 New Canal. After he visited Figsbury Rings outside Salisbury, he wrote about them as Cadbury Rings in *The Longest Journey* (1907).

From 1945 to 1962 William Golding (1911–93) taught English at Bishop Wordsworth's School in the Cathedral Close. It was during this period of his life that he wrote *Lord of the Flies* (1954), his classic novel about a group of schoolboys trapped on a desert island whose society descends into inhumanity. It was his first novel and an instant success. Later, he wrote *The Spire* (1964), which centred on one man's determination to build a massively tall spire for the cathedral despite what anyone else might think of his plans.

Inside Salisbury Cathedral is a memorial window to the poet George Herbert (1593–1633), who was ordained in the cathedral and then became rector of St Andrew in the nearby parish of Bemerton. He wrote much of his poetry in the rectory, and he used to walk over the fields to the cathedral. He died of consumption in 1633 and was buried in the chancel of his church. The stained glass window in his memory was installed in 1953 and was followed by a statue on the west front of the cathedral as part of its millennium project.

ABOVE & OPPOSITE: Many writers have visited Salisbury Cathedral, including Samuel Pepys who used the steeple as a landmark while exploring the town. This steeple was the inspiration for William Golding's *The Spire*.

Coleridge Cottage

NETHER STOWEY, SOMERSET

In 1796, the Romantic poet Samuel Taylor Coleridge (1772–1834) was struggling to support his wife, Sara, their first son, Hartley, and what was

becoming an increasing dependence on opium. Help arrived when his friend, Tom Poole, suggested that Coleridge and his family should come to live next door to him in Lime Street, Nether Stowey. Coleridge needed no prompting, especially as Poole offered him £40 to live on as well. No wonder that Coleridge called him his 'sheet anchor'.

The following June, Coleridge met another man who was to have a major impact on his life. This was William Wordsworth (1770–1850), who soon moved to nearby Alfoxden with his sister, Dorothy. The two

ABOVE & BELOW: Samuel Taylor Coleridge moved into a cottage in Nether Stowey in 1796. It is now named after him. While he lived here he wrote 'The Rime of the Ancient Mariner', among other poems.

poets collaborated on *Lyrical Ballads* (1798), which was a selection of their work.

Wordsworth encouraged Coleridge in his poetry, who subsequently wrote some of his greatest poetry while living at Nether Stowey: 'The Rime of the Ancient Mariner', 'Frost at Midnight' and 'Kubla Khan'. This latter poem was written in 1797 after Coleridge had dosed himself with opium and then fallen asleep while reading about the great Mongolian leader. When he woke, he realized that he had composed more than 200 lines of poetry on the subject while he was asleep, and began to write them down as quickly as possible. Alas, 'a person on business from Porlock' knocked on the door and held him up for an hour, after which he found that the rest of the poem had faded from his memory. He kept the unfinished poem, which was a fragment of what he had dreamed, and it was only published in 1816 at Lord Byron's insistence.

When the Wordsworths had to leave Alfoxden in 1800, Coleridge missed them so much that he and his family followed them to Grasmere in the Lake District (see pages 89–91). Little did he know it, but he was leaving behind one of the happiest periods in his life and the place where he found it easiest to compose his poetry.

Bath

SOMERSET

From the 17th century onwards, Bath was one of the most fashionable cities in the whole of Britain and so it was an important place to be seen, and writers were just as susceptible to the need to be in the vanguard of the latest trend as anyone else. In 1668 the diarist Samuel Pepys (1633–1703) travelled to Bath to take the famous waters, although he was rather dubious about the hygiene of so many naked bodies crowding into one small bathing pool.

Dr Johnson (1709–84), the author of the first dictionary in the English language, visited Bath in 1776, accompanied by his great travelling companions, Hester Thrale (1741–1821) and her husband Henry (c. 1730–1781). The Thrales returned four years later to stay at 14 South Parade, and this time they brought their friend Fanny Burney (1752–1840), who used her experiences of society life as inspiration for her writing. Her first novel, *Evelina*, was published anonymously in 1778.

When Fanny came to Bath she had just been revealed as the author of *Evelina* and was basking in her

new-found celebrity. Three years after the death of Henry Thrale in 1781, Hester married an Italian musician named Gabriel Piozzi in Bath, much to the consternation of her friends, including Dr Johnson and Fanny Burney.

In 1772, Bath's Royal Crescent was the scene of a romantic adventure that inspired Richard Brinsley Sheridan (1751–1816) to write his great comic play *The Rivals*. While living with his parents in New King Street, the young Sheridan fell in love with a singer, Eliza Linley, who lived at 11 Royal Crescent. She was very beautiful, and Sheridan found he had a rival for her affections in one Captain Matthews. To remove her from the path of his opponent, Sheridan carried Eliza off to France. However, Matthews was still smitten by Eliza when she returned to England with Sheridan, who felt duty-bound to fight two duels with Matthews before taking his beloved to London and marrying her. *The Rivals*, which was first performed in 1775, is set in Bath, with Captain Absolute in Sheridan's role and Lydia Languish in that of Eliza's.

The young Thomas De Quincey (1785–1859), the author of *Confessions of an English Opium Eater* (1822), attended Bath Grammar School from 1796–9, while living at 6 Green Park Buildings.

One of the most famous literary associations with Bath is that of Jane Austen. In 1804, following her father's retirement, Jane lived with her parents at 27 Green Park Buildings, during which time she worked on her novel *The Watsons*, which she abandoned after

ABOVE: Several authors and their literary creations have connections with the Royal Crescent in Bath, including Charles Dickens who set some of *The Posthumous Papers of the Pickwick Club* here.

her father's death in 1805. The Austens had previously lived at 1 The Paragon and then 4 Sidney Place. Although Jane had enjoyed spending holidays in Bath, she was less taken with it when she had to live here, and her mischievous pen satirized the city's society in *Persuasion* and *Northanger Abbey*, both of which were published in 1818, a year after her death.

In 1840, Charles Dickens (1812–70) visited his friend, the poet and essayist Walter Savage Landor (1775–1864), who lived at 35 St James Square. It was here that Dickens wrote Little Nell's death scene for *The Old Curiosity Shop* (1841): an event that stunned the story's many avid readers on both sides of the Atlantic. In *Bleak House* (1853) Dickens based the character of Lawrence Boythorne, who had such a passion for litigation, on Landor. According to legend, Bath also figured prominently in another Dickens novel: the proprietor of the London–Bath coach and owner of the now-demolished White Hart Hotel in Stall Street was one Moses Pickwick, who gave his name to Samuel Pickwick in *The Posthumous Papers of the Pickwick Club* (1837). In the novel, Mr Pickwick and his fellow members of the Pickwick Club stay at Bath, first at the White Hart Hotel and then in Royal Crescent.

CHAPTER 2

South-east England

RUDYARD KIPLING

Perhaps because of its proximity to London, the south-east of England has a great many literary connections. The gentle undulations of the South Downs have attracted writers for centuries, from John Evelyn, who grew up in Lewes, to Alfred, Lord Tennyson who loved to walk through the Surrey lanes. Sussex became the home-from-home of the Bloomsbury Group, centred round Virginia and Leonard Woolf's house in Rodmell, while Hampshire has strong links with Jane Austen. Kent is forever connected with Charles Dickens, who loved the county and put many Kentish characters and places into his novels. And the holiday resort town of Brighton has drawn writers from Dr Johnson to Graham Greene, while George Orwell, Cyril Connolly and Rumer Godden all went to school in Eastbourne.

CHARLES DICKENS

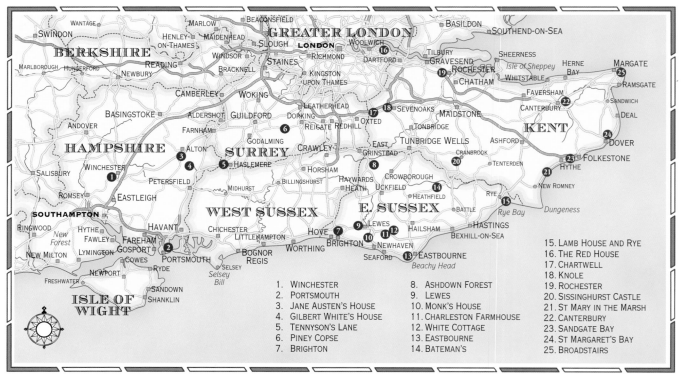

1. WINCHESTER
2. PORTSMOUTH
3. JANE AUSTEN'S HOUSE
4. GILBERT WHITE'S HOUSE
5. TENNYSON'S LANE
6. PINEY COPSE
7. BRIGHTON

8. ASHDOWN FOREST
9. LEWES
10. MONK'S HOUSE
11. CHARLESTON FARMHOUSE
12. WHITE COTTAGE
13. EASTBOURNE
14. BATEMAN'S

15. LAMB HOUSE AND RYE
16. THE RED HOUSE
17. CHARTWELL
18. KNOLE
19. ROCHESTER
20. SISSINGHURST CASTLE
21. ST MARY IN THE MARSH
22. CANTERBURY
23. SANDGATE BAY
24. ST MARGARET'S BAY
25. BROADSTAIRS

ABOVE: By the time Jane Austen died and was buried in Winchester Cathedral in 1817 she was a very popular author. She dedicated *Emma* to her great fan, the Prince Regent.

PREVIOUS PAGE: Bateman's Mill stands in the grounds of Bateman's, where Rudyard Kipling lived from 1902. He fitted the water-mill with a turbine to supply the house with electricity.

Winchester

HAMPSHIRE

When Jane Austen died in her lodgings at 8 College Street in Winchester in July 1817, she was such a celebrated writer that she was given the posthumous honour of being buried in Winchester Cathedral. Her grave is in the north aisle of the nave, and is marked with a stone tablet and a memorial window.

Jane was following in illustrious footsteps, as Izaak Walton (1593–1683) was buried in the south transept of the cathedral, in Prior Silkstede's Chapel. Although Walton wrote biographies of several important figures, including the poets John Donne (1572–1631) and George Herbert, it is *The Compleat Angler* that has gained literary immortality. It was first published in 1653 and then greatly revised for the second edition two years later.

Winchester's Cathedral Library is maintained in the oldest book room in Europe, having been added to the cathedral in the 12th century. It contains a first edition of Gilbert White's *The Natural History and Antiquities of Selborne*, which was published in 1789 (see page 28), as well as a copy of the speech that Sir Walter Ralegh made from the scaffold in 1618.

When the poet John Keats (1795–1821) visited Winchester in the summer and early autumn of 1819, while staying with his friend Charles Armitage Brown, he commented that 'the side streets here are excessively maiden-lady-like'. The city was also familiar to Anthony Trollope, who attended Winchester College for a short time before going to Harrow in 1827. He later based *The Warden* (1855), which was the first of his Barsetshire novels and concerns the strangely comfortable life of the warden of Hiram's Hospital, on a similar scandal that surrounded the master of Winchester's Hospital of St Cross in 1808. In 1837, ten years after Trollope was at Winchester, the young Matthew Arnold (1822–88) was a pupil at the college before he was sent to Rugby (see pages 75–6), where his father was headmaster.

Portsmouth

HAMPSHIRE

In February 1812, the great Victorian novelist Charles Dickens was born at 1 Mile End Terrace, which is now the Charles Dickens Birthplace Museum, 393 Commercial Road. His father, John, was a clerk in the Navy Pay Office. Money was tight and that June the family had to move to a smaller house, 18 Hawke Street, which has since been demolished. They stayed here for the next two years until John Dickens was given a post in London. Charles Dickens returned to Portsmouth in 1838 when he was writing *Nicholas Nickleby* (1839), and in the novel the title character and his companion, Smike, appear at the local theatre with the Crummles theatrical company.

Portsmouth also played an important role in the life of Sir Arthur Conan Doyle (1859–1930). In 1882 he first began to practise as a doctor in the town, and this was also where he created the character of Sherlock

Holmes, who was based on Dr Joseph Bell who had taught Doyle medicine at Edinburgh University. Dr Watson, who narrates the Sherlock Holmes stories, was based on Dr James Watson, a friend of Doyle's, who was the President of the Portsmouth Literary and Scientific Society. Doyle left Portsmouth for Vienna in 1889, by which time he had written *A Study in Scarlet* (1887), *Micah Clarke* (1889), *The Sign of Four* (1890) and *The White Company* (1891).

Jane Austen's House

CHAWTON, HAMPSHIRE

When Jane Austen, her widowed mother and her sister, Cassandra, moved to Chawton in July 1809, they chose it because it was near Chawton Manor, which was owned by Jane's newly widowed brother, Edward. Their house was called Chawton Cottage.

It was here that Jane wrote the final versions of her novels. Space was limited so she had to write in the sitting room she shared with her mother and sister, and she would hastily tidy away her papers whenever anyone entered the room – the creaky sitting room door gave her adequate warning of someone's approach.

If the circumstances of Jane's life – living in a small country cottage with her widowed mother and younger sister – sound uncannily like those of the two sisters in *Sense and Sensibility* (1811), it is hardly surprising as this was the first novel of hers to be published. However, its gestation had taken a long time as Jane began it in 1795 when it was much shorter and had the simple title, *Elinor and Marianne*.

More novels followed. *Pride and Prejudice*, which began life as *First Impressions* in 1797 but was later heavily reworked, was published in 1813. Jane also wrote new novels at Chawton – *Mansfield Park* (1814), *Emma* (1816), *Persuasion* (1818) and *Northanger Abbey* (1818). The latter two works were published after her death in Winchester (see page 26) at the age of 42. She was ill at Chawton for some time before her death, and was aware that illness did not suit her. In characteristic style, when commenting on her changed appearance, she said 'Sickness is a dangerous Indulgence at my time of Life'.

BELOW: Chawton Cottage, where Jane Austen lived from 1809, is now a museum devoted to her memory.

ABOVE: What began as a series of letters to his friends about the delights of his home grew into Gilbert White's book *The Natural History and Antiquities of Selborne*.

Gilbert White's House

SELBORNE, HAMPSHIRE

Selborne is synonymous with the naturalist Gilbert White (1720–93), who was born in the vicarage and spent most of his life in the village. He lived at The Wakes, which is now called Gilbert White's House and Garden, from 1751 until his death. He loved the abundance of nature that he was able to observe in his garden and the surrounding countryside, and this inspired him to begin writing the letters about his observations that were eventually collected in his book, *The Natural History and Antiquities of Selborne* (1789). The recipients of his letters were two other naturalists, Thomas Pennant and Daines Barrington, and their correspondence began in 1767. Pennant was also an author, whose tours of Scotland, Wales and the Hebrides were published in the 1770s.

After White's death he was buried to the north of the chancel in Selborne churchyard. The very simple headstone bears only his initials and the date of his death, so can easily be missed.

Tennyson's Lane

HASLEMERE, SURREY

By the time Alfred Tennyson (1809–92) and his wife, Emily, moved to Haslemere in 1869, Tennyson had reached the height of his fame and more modern poets were snapping at his heels. He had been Poet Laureate since 1851, following the death of William Wordsworth, and was a great favourite of Queen Victoria. She felt an especial empathy for him after the death of her husband, Prince Albert, in 1861, when she took great comfort from Tennyson's epic poem, *In Memoriam* (1850), which dealt with his grief following the death of his great friend, Arthur Hallam.

In 1865, the Tennysons moved to a farmhouse near

28

Haslemere. They had spent many years living at Farringford (now a hotel), in Freshwater on the Isle of Wight, but it was becoming too busy with sightseers who wanted a glimpse of the poet, and from now on they divided their time between the island and Surrey. They bought some land in Surrey and started to build their new home, Aldworth (which was named after Emily's family home in Berkshire) near the summit of Blackdown. Tennyson was able to relax, garden, entertain friends and enjoy family life here. He particularly enjoyed walking around the neighbouring countryside, and Tennyson's Lane is named for him.

Tennyson continued to write and experimented with plays, although he noted that 'the worst of writing for the stage is, you must always keep some actor in your mind'. Although he had twice been offered a baronetcy and refused it, he finally agreed at the third time of asking in 1884, and became Baron Tennyson of Aldworth and Farringford. Tennyson died at Aldworth in October 1892, having read Shakespeare's *Cymbeline* only a few hours before his death. The book was placed in his coffin and he was buried in Westminster Abbey with the full weight of Victorian pomp and ceremony.

ABOVE & OPPOSITE, BELOW: Tennyson and his wife bought land in Haslemere, where one of his favourite walks was renamed Tennyson's Lane.

ABINGER, SURREY

E.M. Forster, who wrote so evocatively of Italy in *A Room with a View* (1908) and of India in *A Passage to India* (1924), had a long-standing affection for the quintessentially English countryside around Abinger in Surrey. This was where he grew up and where his father built a house for his sister, Laura. When Laura died in April 1924 she left the house, West Hackhurst, to Forster.

Soon after Forster inherited the house, he learned that the adjoining wood, Piney Copse, was under threat and so he bought it. His neighbour, Lord Farrer, had wanted to buy the wood but graciously accepted defeat – at the time. Many of the trees had been felled during the First World War so Forster set about replanting the wood. He opened Piney Copse for the annual treat of the local school and wrote an essay about it, 'My Wood', for the *New Leader* in 1926.

Forster loved West Hackhurst and Piney Copse, but there was a fly in this rural ointment: the house was leasehold and the freeholder, who was none other than Lord Farrer, was equivocal about whether he would extend the very short lease. When the time came to negotiate, Lord Farrer agreed to renew the lease on the condition that Forster sold him Piney Copse. Forster decided to spike Farrer's guns by offering to leave Piney Copse to the National Trust after his death, so he lost West Hackhurst.

Only a few miles away is Box Hill, which is the scene of one of Mrs Elton's 'exploring parties' in Jane Austen's *Emma* (1816).

ABOVE: Piney Copse was E.M. Forster's beloved stretch of woodland near West Hackhurst, his house in Abinger.

BELOW: In Graham Greene's *Brighton Rock*, Hale was murdered by Pinkie while enjoying the delights of the Palace Pier.

Brighton

SUSSEX

The seaside resort of Brighton was firmly put on the social map at the end of the 18th century when the Prince of Wales, later George IV (1820–30), visited the town and took a liking to it. It had previously been a fishing village called Brighthelmstone, but with the Prince's patronage it began to go up in the world.

In the 1770s, Hester and Henry Thrale took a house in West Street for the summer holidays, and soon their great friend Dr Samuel Johnson was joining them on their annual visits to the Sussex coast. During one trip, Dr Johnson was busy working on *The Lives of the English Poets* (1781), which was one of his great literary achievements. When Johnson was commissioned to write the book, the plan was that he should write biographical prefaces to the selected poems of 52 English poets, but such was his fame that when it was published the book consisted solely of his prefaces. The Thrales also entertained Fanny Burney in Brighton. The couple took her to the Assembly Rooms, which were attached to the Old Ship Inn in Ship Street.

The Thrales' house was later knocked down and replaced by a concert hall at which Charles Dickens gave his celebrated readings from his novels. Dickens was no stranger to Brighton, or to the Old Ship Inn where he sometimes stayed. He also stayed at 62 East Street, 148 Kings Road and at the Bedford Hotel where he wrote parts of *Dombey and Son* (1848). Some of this book is set in Brighton; Mrs Pipchin, 'a bitter old lady', keeps a children's boarding house here, where the Dombey children have the misfortune to stay.

Brighton also appears in *Pride and Prejudice* (1813) by Jane Austen; *Vanity Fair* (1848) by William Thackeray (1811–63); *Rodney Stone* (1896) by Arthur Conan Doyle; *Clayhanger* (1910) and *Hilda Lessways* (1911) by Arnold Bennett (1867–1931); *Of Human Bondage* (1915) by Somerset Maugham (1874–1965) and, of course, *Brighton Rock* (1938) by Graham Greene (1904–91). Greene's novel concentrated on the seedy side of Brighton, a world of gang warfare, casual sex and emotional cruelty. Greene later painted a happier, breezier side of the town in *Travels with my Aunt* (1969).

Ashdown Forest

EAST SUSSEX

Fans of A.A. Milne's *Winnie-the-Pooh* stories should have no difficulty in recognizing the landscape of Ashdown Forest because it forms such a startling resemblance to Hundred Acre Wood, where Pooh, Piglet and their friends played with Christopher Robin. Here are the lofty Scots pines straight from the illustrations by E.H. Shepard, with their bare trunks topped by little sprouts of green. Here also, if you care to scramble through the woods to find it, is the original Poohsticks Bridge where Pooh and his friends saw Eeyore floating past while playing their favourite game, which involved dropping a stick into the river and waiting to see whose sailed under the bridge first.

A.A. Milne (1882–1956) knew the area well because he and his family spent their summer holidays here each year. They stayed at Cotchford Farm, which is on the edge of the village of Upper Hartfield, and Milne's young son – always known to his family as Billy Moon but known to the rest of the world by his real name of Christopher Robin – explored the woods, sand pits and lanes around Ashdown Forest. Although Milne was a prolific playwright he will always be famous for the four books he wrote in the 1920s about the adventures of his young son and his toys: *When We Were Very Young* (1924); *Winnie-the-Pooh* (1926); *Now We Are Six* (1927) and *The House at Pooh Corner* (1928).

In his two autobiographies, *The Enchanted Places* (1974) and *The Path through the Trees* (1979), Christopher Milne (1920–96) gave a somewhat less idyllic account of his childhood than might be imagined from reading his father's books. Nevertheless, his books link many of the places in Ashdown Forest with those that appear in his father's stories, so are a fascinating guide for anyone who wants to discover the sites of *Winnie-the-Pooh* for themselves.

Lewes

EAST SUSSEX

John Evelyn (1620–1706), the 17th-century diarist whose journals tell us so much about the world he inhabited, first came to Lewes when he was a small boy. He stayed with his maternal grandparents, the

ABOVE: The original Poohsticks Bridge in Ashdown Forest has been preserved, although it is so popular that it can be difficult to find any sticks with which to play the eponymous game.

Stansfields, so he could attend school in the town. He was first taught by a Mr Potts in the Cliffe, and then moved on to the Grammar School in 1630. This was very convenient for young John because it backed onto Southover Grange, the Elizabethan house that was his grandmother's new home after her remarriage following her first husband's death.

Southover Grange was later transformed into Mock Beggars Hall when William Harrison Ainsworth (1805–82) chose it as the setting for his Civil War novel *Ovingdean Grange – A Tale of the South Downs* (1860). He wrote 30 novels, most of them historical, and lived in nearby Brighton. Although Southover Grange now houses council offices, the gardens are open to the public.

In the 1760s, the upper room in the White Hart Hotel, in Lewes's High Street, was home to the Headstrong Club. This consisted of a group of men who were dissatisfied with the status quo, one of which was Thomas Paine (1737–1809). Paine was born in Thetford, Norfolk, the son of a corset-marker, and, after a rudimentary education, he became an exciseman. This career was unsuccessful, not helped by the fact that he complained loudly about the pay and working conditions of life in Customs and Excise.

Paine lived at Bull House in Lewes High Street, having married the daughter of his landlord. For a while he helped to run the family tobacconist's shop, until he and his wife separated. He went to Philadelphia in 1774, on the advice of the American statesman Benjamin Franklin (1706–90), whom he'd met in London in 1774. There, his life was transformed from one of frustrated rebellion to that of a writer at the very forefront of the revolution that was sweeping through the American colonies. Paine began to write political pamphlets that were literary dynamite; his *African Slavery in America*, which was strongly anti-slavery, was published in 1775, followed by *Common Sense* in 1776, which championed American independence from Britain. He later wrote his two greatest works: *The Rights of Man* (1791) and *The Age of Reason* (1793).

In July 1919, the White Hart was the scene of another literary event when Leonard Woolf (1880–1969) attended a house auction there and bought Monk's House (see below) in Rodmell for £700. This was highly inconvenient, as he and his wife, Virginia, had only recently bought the Round House in Lewes but were already finding fault with it. Much against their wishes, they had discovered that they could not fault Monk's House as a residence and immediately fell in love with it. They sold the Lewes house and moved to Rodmell, which became their life-long home.

We giggle and joke, and go and poke at roots and plan beds of nasturtiums.

VIRGINIA WOOLF

ABOVE: Cyril Connolly, who lived in nearby Eastbourne, often enjoyed lunch at The White Hart Hotel in Lewes.
OPPOSITE: Virginia Woolf loved the countryside around Lewes and had three consecutive homes here.

Monk's House

RODMELL, EAST SUSSEX

It took three attempts for Virginia Woolf to find the house she wanted in Sussex. She began looking for what she hoped would be a suitable retreat from London in 1911, when she rented a house in West Firle, just outside Lewes. Virginia was not keen on the house, which she named Little Talland House, but loved the countryside, and in the spring of 1912 she took a five-year lease on Asheham House, off the London–Seaford road. Soon after this, Virginia married Leonard Woolf, and they enjoyed living at Asheham until 1919 when the lease expired. They bought Monk's House, in Rodmell, which was such a simple cottage that it lacked a lavatory, hot water and bath. Such privations were soon remedied, and the Woolfs established a comfortable domestic routine that Virginia described vividly in her many letters and diaries. Leonard gardened or wrote while Virginia composed her novels and did her best to manage their rather unpredictable servants, Nelly and Lottie.

Despite being inferior in many ways to Asheham House, Monk's House had two great advantages. It offered Virginia the chance to enjoy some wonderful walks along the banks of the River Ouse, and it was close to Charleston (see below), which was the Sussex home of her adored sister, Vanessa, and her family.

Monk's House quickly became filled with the Woolfs' many friends. One of the first visitors was T.S. Eliot (1888–1965), whose poems had just been published by the Hogarth Press, which was owned and run by Virginia and Leonard. Other writers, including E.M. Forster, Lytton Strachey and Vita Sackville-West (1892–1962), with whom Virginia had an intimate friendship and possibly a sexual affair, were frequent visitors.

Although Virginia enjoyed entertaining her friends and valued the joys of conversation above many other pleasures, her fragile physical and mental health meant that her social life always had to be restricted to some extent. She had several nervous breakdowns, which often coincided with the publication of a new novel, and she became increasingly anxious about the critical reception of her work. Leonard always supported her during these extremely difficult phases, but was unable to help her in 1941 when she became very ill through fear about the worth of *Between the Acts*, which she had just completed. Afraid that her intermittent madness was returning she made the decision to kill herself, and on 28 March 1941 she wrote farewell letters to Leonard and Vanessa, loaded her pockets with heavy stones and drowned herself in the River Ouse.

Leonard and Vanessa had the horror of having to wait for three weeks before Virginia's body was found. She was cremated and her ashes were buried under one of the two tall elms in the garden at Monk's House. Leonard continued to live and write at Monk's House until his death in 1969, and was a much-loved member of the village throughout that time.

Charleston Farmhouse

FIRLE, EAST SUSSEX

In 1916, Virginia Woolf found what she hoped would be a suitable home for her sister, the artist Vanessa Bell (1879–1961), and her family. Although Vanessa was married to Clive Bell, she was now living with the painter, Duncan Grant (1885–1978), who was anxious to avoid being sent to fight in the First World War. He had become a full-time agricultural worker in Suffolk in order to escape conscription, and when he and Vanessa moved to Charleston Farm in Firle, a

village just outside Lewes, he once again worked for a neighbouring farmer. His friend and former lover, David Garnett (1892–1981), also moved from Suffolk to Sussex, where he too worked on the land.

Charleston soon became a popular country retreat for many members of the Bloomsbury Group (see page 54). Virginia and her husband, Leonard, lived nearby at Monk's House (see pages 32–33), and the two households, complete with guests, visited each other as often as possible. Life at Charleston was relaxed and Bohemian, and attracted such visitors as the art critic Roger Fry (1866–1934), E.M. Forster, Lytton Strachey (1880–1932) and Frances Partridge (1900–2004), who wrote about her visits in her series of memoirs drawn from her diaries. The writer and economist, John Maynard Keynes (1883–1946), another former lover of Duncan Grant, who was now married to the Russian ballerina, Lydia Lopokova (1892–1981), lived nearby at Tilton Farm.

To outsiders, the occupants of Charleston were always perceived as highly unconventional. When Vanessa's daughter, Angelica, was born in 1918, David Garnett wrote that he might marry her one day, which he did in 1942 after the death of his first wife, Ray. Angelica Garnett wrote vividly of her childhood and life at Charleston in her memoir, *Deceived with Kindness* (1984).

Charleston continued to be a thriving artistic and literary community for many years until Duncan Grant died in 1978, when the house was opened to the public. It has become such a popular attraction that it now hosts the Charleston Literary Festival each year, which attracts many famous literary names.

White Cottage

RIPE, EAST SUSSEX

In January 1956, Margerie Lowry found White Cottage in Ripe, a tiny village in the maze of country lanes that lie to the east of Lewes. It was exactly what she had been looking for – somewhere peaceful and rural, where her husband, the novelist Malcolm Lowry

(1909–57), could rebuild his life and career, but which nevertheless was near the regular medical help he needed for his alcoholism and manic depression.

Malcolm Lowry was desperately trying to pick up the threads of his tattered writing career. After the acclaim that accompanied *Under the Volcano* (1947), which was set in Mexico and chronicled the last few hours of the British ex-consul Geoffrey Firmin on the Day of the Dead, Lowry struggled to write anything that would be a worthy successor to it. He was greatly hindered by his mental problems and his chronic alcoholism, but strongly supported by his second wife, Margerie, who was also a writer.

Lowry was able to write again in Ripe – it probably helped that he was banned from the local pub, The Lamb – but he died in June 1957, after getting drunk and starting a fight with his wife. She ran to a neighbour to ask for help, but when she returned Lowry was dead. He was buried in the churchyard at Ripe, as was Margerie in 1988, although their graves are not together. Among his books that were published posthumously are *Hear Us O Lord from Heaven Thy Dwelling Place* (1961) and *October Ferry to Gabriola* (1970).

Eastbourne

EAST SUSSEX

For thousands of holidaymakers, Eastbourne is a place of happiness and relaxation. But for the young Eric Arthur Blair, who later wrote under the pseudonym George Orwell (1903–50), it was a place that filled him with dread. He was sent to St Cyprian's, which was a prep school for boys that seems to have attracted more than its fair share of pupils who went on to become celebrated artists. Among its alumni were the photographer Cecil Beaton (1904–80) and the writers Cyril Connolly (1903–74) and Gavin Maxwell (1914–69). Orwell wrote of his schooldays in Eastbourne in his essay, 'Such, Such were the Joys', which was published posthumously and takes the school to task for the privations and cruelties that he had to endure there.

Connolly also wrote about the school in *Enemies of Promise* (1938), but took the precaution of renaming it St Wulfric's. Despite this flimsy disguise, the piece provoked a reproachful letter from Mrs Wilkes, the headmistress who was universally known to her charges as Flip. His childhood experiences of the town did not deter Connolly from moving here in 1968. He bought 48 St John's Road, close to the South Downs, and wrote to a friend 'Eastbourne is heaven'. John Betjeman agreed, writing to him, 'Eastbourne is the right place for a man of letters.' After his death in November 1974 Connolly was buried in Berwick Church, at the foot of the downs.

Another man of letters who was attracted to Eastbourne was Charles Lutwidge Dodgson (1832–98), perhaps better known as Lewis Carroll, who spent each summer holiday at 7 Lushington Road between 1877 and 1887. His first children's novel, *Alice's Adventures in Wonderland*, was published in 1865 and his second, *Through the Looking-Glass and What Alice Found There*, in 1871. Carroll wrote some of this latter book in the summerhouse while staying at the vicarage in Selmeston, a small village between Eastbourne and Lewes.

Rumer Godden (1907–98), who wrote *Black Narcissus* (1939) and *The Greengage Summer* (1958) among many other novels, was born in Eastbourne and described the town as 'the most dreadful place'. Her family took her to India shortly after she was born, but in 1920 she and her sisters were sent back to school in England. It took five attempts for them to find a school they were happy with, eventually settling on Moira House, a private school for girls in Eastbourne. One of the teachers, Miss Swann, encouraged Rumer to write, for which she was always grateful.

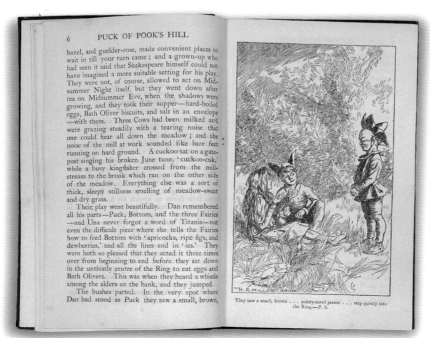

They saw a small, brown . . . pointy-eared person . . . step quietly into the Ring.—P. 6.

ABOVE: Bateman's was Rudyard Kipling's cherished home for more than 30 years. It has been preserved as he knew it, full of books, paintings and other Kipling memorabilia.
OPPOSITE: Kipling wrote *Puck of Pook's Hill* about two children who manage to make Puck materialize on Midsummer's Eve.

Bateman's

BURWASH, EAST SUSSEX

'That's She! The only She! Make an honest woman of her, quick!' This, Rudyard Kipling (1865–1936) recorded in his autobiography, *Something of Myself for My Friends Known and Unknown* (1937), was how he and his wife, Carrie, felt the first time they visited Bateman's in 1902. The 17th-century house offered them the peace and solitude they were looking for, and they lived here for the rest of their lives.

The Kiplings moved to Bateman's from Rottingdean, which is on the Sussex coast just east of Brighton. Their life there, at a house called The Elms, had become tainted with grief after the death of their seven-year-old daughter, Josephine. It was also rendered intolerable by all the tourists from Brighton who flocked to the village in the hope of catching a glimpse of Kipling, who had achieved considerable fame.

Life at Bateman's promised to be different. Here they could bury themselves in the Sussex Weald and Kipling could continue his prodigious output of stories and poems relatively undisturbed, working in his study. The tranquil setting of the house, and what he felt to be its good Feng Shui, inspired some of his greatest works, including *Rewards and Fairies* (1910), which contains his most famous poem, 'If', and *Puck of Pook's Hill* (1906). Pook's Hill is visible from the house.

Tragedy struck in 1915 when the Kiplings' only son, John, was killed in action at the Battle of Loos. After this event, much of Kipling's writing focused on war and its repercussions. The shock of his son's death

ABOVE: E.F. Benson loved Lamb House so much that he turned it into Mallards in his Tilling novels. He would still recognize the house, but his beloved Garden Room was destroyed in the Second World War.

coincided with the onset of a gastric ulcer that eventually killed him in 1936. Carrie died in 1940 and bequeathed Bateman's to the National Trust. It has been kept as it would have been when the Kiplings were alive, and displays the Nobel Prize for Literature that was awarded to the writer in 1907.

Lamb House and Rye

EAST SUSSEX

'It's astonishing how, within and without, everything wears and how, even now I discover new charm in the familiar and new assurances in the usual.' So wrote Henry James (1843–1916) about his beloved Lamb House, where he lived from 1897 until his death. In the summer he worked in the Garden Room, which stood at right angles to the house, and in the winter he moved inside to the Green Room upstairs. James wrote three of his greatest novels – *The Wings of the Dove* (1902), *The Ambassadors* (1903) and *The Golden Bowl* (1904) – in the house, and made it Mr Longdon's home in *The Awkward Age* (1899).

James entertained a coterie of literary colleagues here, including fellow novelists H.G. Wells (1866–1946), Rudyard Kipling, Joseph Conrad (1857–1924) and Edith Wharton (1862–1937). If his guests arrived by train they were met at Rye station by James and his gardener, who carried their luggage to the house in his wheelbarrow; as Rye is chiefly composed of steep, cobbled streets this must have been quite a feat.

Rheumatism prevented James from writing in longhand so he dictated his novels to his secretary, and while navigating his way through the lengthy sentences for which he is so well known, he would gaze out of the window of the Garden Room to see what was happening. This room was also a favourite haunt of E.F. Benson (1867–1940), who was the next tenant of Lamb House. He moved here in 1919 and stayed until he died in 1940.

Benson drew heavily on Lamb House for his series of novels about Tilling, which was Rye in an almost non-existent disguise. Lamb House became Mallards, the so-called ancestral home of the formidable Miss Elizabeth Mapp, before unwise speculations on the Stock Exchange forced her to relinquish it to her arch rival, Mrs Emmeline Lucas, popularly known as Lucia. Both characters would spy on the street from the Garden Room, and Lucia took particular delight in her *giardino segreto*, as she called it, whereas Benson knew this little piece of garden as his 'secret garden'. Rye's Mermaid Street became Porpoise Street, although the Landgate retained its real name. It was from here one Boxing Day that all of Tilling watched with horror as Mapp and Lucia were swept out to sea on an upturned kitchen table.

In 1935, Benson had a lookout built near the Landgate, which has views over the stretch of marsh that his heroines would have sailed over; a plaque exists today to mark this site. Benson also used his own experiences for the novels. In *Trouble for Lucia* (1939), Lucia became Mayor of Tilling, an office she shared with her creator who was Major of Rye from 1934 to 1937.

Benson had many friends and enjoyed mixing with his neighbouring writers. A fellow novelist in Rye was Radclyffe Hall (1883–1943), who had proclaimed her lesbianism in her ground-breaking novel, *The Well of*

Loneliness (1928), which was immediately banned and not republished until 1949. She lived with her lover, Una, Lady Troubridge, in the High Street and felt that Benson was letting the side down by not being open about his own homosexuality.

Rumer Godden was the tenant of Lamb House from 1968–74. By this time, the house was the property of the National Trust. She wrote of her experiences here in her autobiography, *The House with Four Rooms* (1989).

The Red House

BEXLEYHEATH, GREATER LONDON

When William Morris (1834–96) and his wife Jane (1839–1914) moved to the Red House in 1859 it was the start of Morris's career as a textile and furniture designer, and as co-founder of the Arts and Crafts Movement, although he did not know it at the time. Frustration at being unable to find any decent furniture for their new home led Morris to found the design firm Morris, Marshall, Faulkener and Co. Their work in textile and furniture design had a revolutionary impact on the Victorian way of life.

William and Jane had just married when they moved into the Red House, which was built for them by fellow designer Philip Webb. Morris had secured a personal triumph by marrying Jane Burden, who was one of the most popular models for the Pre-Raphaelite painters. Her beauty and popularity led to problems between them as Jane later had an affair with Morris's long-standing friend, Dante Gabriel Rossetti (1828–82).

Morris was a writer as well as a designer, and when he moved to the Red House he had just published *The Defence of Guenevere and other poems* (1858).

He later founded the Kelmscott Press, which published many of his books.

William and Jane sold the Red House after living here for five years and moved to Queen Street, in Holborn, London. The Red House remained in private hands until it was acquired by the National Trust and opened to the public in 2003.

Chartwell

WESTERHAM, KENT

Winston Churchill (1874–1965) and his wife, Clementine (1885–1977), moved to Chartwell in 1924. Churchill had bought the house in 1922, rather against his wife's wishes, and although he continued to love it throughout his life it never gave Clementine the same pleasure.

Chartwell became Churchill's solace and inspiration, especially during the Second World War when he had the unenviable task of being Prime Minister. He would gaze through his bedroom window at the Weald of

BELOW: William Morris's Red House is now open to the public. During renovation, a wall painting by Lizzie Siddall, wife of Dante Gabriel Rossetti, was discovered behind a cupboard.

Kent spread out before him and gather strength from the view – it was land like this that Britain was fighting for.

Although Chartwell was usually full of people, whether family, personal friends or political allies, Churchill also found time to write here. He was a prolific author and his work included the six volumes of *The Second World War* (1948–54) as well as the four volumes of *A History of the English-speaking Peoples* (1956–8).

After Churchill's death in January 1965, Clementine decided that she would give Chartwell to the National Trust after her own death. The house has been left as it was when the Churchills lived here, complete with many of their possessions, which include some of Churchill's paintings and the wall he built in the garden.

Knole

SEVENOAKS, KENT

It was one of the great tragedies in the life of Vita Sackville-West (1892–1962) that her sex prevented her inheriting Knole, which is where she was born and was her beloved childhood home. She was the only child of the 3rd Lord Sackville and, much to her distress, when he died the title and Knole passed to her cousin, Eddy Sackville-West. Vita had always been a tomboy, which made the British rules of primogeniture even harder to bear.

Any child growing up in such an atmospheric old house would be impressed by its scale, beauty and grandeur, but Knole made a particularly strong impact on Vita, who had a strong aesthetic sense, a love of

history and a powerful imagination. In later life, when she had become established as a poet and novelist (writing as V. Sackville-West), she drew heavily on her memories of Knole. The King's Bedroom, filled with solid silver furniture for a visit from James I of England and left virtually untouched ever since, was where Vita had first been properly kissed by Harold Nicolson (1886–1968), who became her husband, and where she later took other lovers.

In *The Edwardians* (1930), Knole becomes Chevron, and the King's Bedroom is the room where Sebastian tries to seduce the doctor's wife. Vita also wrote a biography of the house, *Knole and the Sackvilles* (1923), into which she was able to pour her love and knowledge of her ancestral home.

The heady combination of Knole and Vita fired the imagination of Virginia Woolf, who was inspired to write *Orlando* (1928) about them both. At the time, the two women were conducting a passionate friendship, and the novel is essentially Virginia's greatest love letter to Vita. It is crammed with incidents and people from Vita's life, and covers four centuries from its Elizabethan beginnings to its end on 11 October 1928, which was the publication day. Virginia gave the manuscript to Vita, who presented it to Knole.

Knole itself had already had experience of writers before Vita lived there. Thomas Sackville (1536–1608), the 1st Earl of Dorset, was a writer, and the 3rd Earl entertained the playwrights Sir Francis Beaumont

BELOW: Vita Sackville-West never lost her love for Knole, where she grew up. After her cousin inherited the house, Vita sometimes took moonlit walks through the grounds without telling him.

(1584–1616), John Fletcher (1579–1625) and Ben Jonson (c. 1572–1637) and the poet John Donne (1572–1631) here. Donne used to preach in the chapel at Knole each year during his annual visit to his nearby parish church of St Nicholas in Sevenoaks. The 3rd Countess of Dorset was often moved to tears by Donne's sermons.

Rochester

KENT

Charles Dickens knew Rochester well as a boy and, in common with other places in Kent, it inspired many of his novels. In *The Posthumous Papers of the Pickwick Club* (1837), that comic scoundrel, Mr Jingle, describes Rochester Castle in his characteristic, telegraphic style: 'Ah, fine place!… glorious pile – frowning walls – tottering arches – dark nooks – crumbling staircases.' Mr Pickwick stayed at the Bull Hotel, which is now the Royal Victoria and Bull Inn. The streets are crammed with many other reminders of favourite Dickens characters, such as Restoration House in Crow Lane, which was the model for Miss Havisham's cobweb-infested home in *Great Expectations* (1861). Eastgate House Museum in the High Street became the Nun's House, which was Miss Twinkleton's Seminary for Young Ladies in *The Mystery of Edwin Drood* (1870), in which Rochester itself was transformed into Cloisterham.

The Swiss chalet in which Dickens wrote several of his later books is now in the garden of Eastgate House. It was originally assembled in the garden at Gad's Hill (now a school), which was Dickens' home from 1856 until his death there in 1870. He had always loved Gad's Hill as a boy, and his father told him encouragingly that he might eventually own it if he worked hard enough. Dickens was certainly no stranger to hard work and he was able to buy the house in 1856, having heard quite by chance that it was coming on to the market. It was his holiday home until September 1860 when he made it his permanent residence.

One of the first guests in 1856 was Hans Christian Andersen (1805–75), the children's author. However, the visit was not an unparalleled success. Dickens wrote that his family were 'suffering a good deal from Andersen' because it was so difficult to understand

ABOVE: Restoration House in Crow Lane, Rochester, was renamed Satis House by Dickens in *Great Expectations* in which it was the neglected home of the jilted Miss Havisham.

what he was saying.

Dickens died on the dining room sofa at Gad's Hill on 9 June 1870, having had a stroke the day before after spending hours writing *Edwin Drood*. There is a curious coincidence about the date of his death because exactly five years before, on 9 June 1865, he and his mistress, Ellen Ternan, were involved in a serious railway accident at Staplehurst in Kent. Dickens took care of many of the casualties before suddenly remembering that he had left the latest chapter of *Our Mutual Friend* (1865) in the railway compartment, and clambered back in to retrieve it. Once safely back at Gad's Hill he suffered from delayed shock and never fully recovered.

Sissinghurst Castle

CRANBROOK, KENT

Vita Sackville-West wanted to be remembered as a poet and writer, but feared that instead she would remain in the public's collective memory

ABOVE: Vita Sackville-West devoted herself to her two great loves – gardening and writing – at Sissinghurst. She was delighted to discover that it had once been owned by her family, the Sackvilles.

and journalist; his works include *Some People* (1927) and his three volumes of diaries (1966–68). When not in London, Harold wrote on the ground floor of the South Cottage, while Vita worked in a room halfway up the tower in a different part of the garden.

The tower was Vita's private domain, where she was able to satisfy her innate need for seclusion and reclusiveness, and where she could work on her books and poetry. These included her biography of St Theresa of Avila and St Therese of Lisieux, *The Eagle and the Dove* (1943), and her long poem *The Garden* (1946). Both the tower and the garden were Vita's refuge whenever a love affair became too complicated or when her chronic shyness and incipient loneliness overwhelmed her.

Very few people were allowed to cross the threshold of her writing room, and her sons, Nigel and Ben, were even forbidden to climb the spiral staircase that led to it. Whenever Vita was wanted for a meal or a telephone call, she was called from the foot of the staircase in the opposite turret: she could not be fetched in person. Even now, the many thousands of visitors who throng to Sissinghurst each year are only allowed to peer through the wrought-iron gate which blocks the doorway of the writing room.

The original printing press with which Virginia and Leonard Woolf began the Hogarth Press, and who became Vita's publishers, is also on display at Sissinghurst.

St Mary in the Marsh

DYMCHURCH, KENT

The quiet beauty and huge skies of Romney Marsh have attracted many writers over the centuries. One of the most celebrated residents was E. Nesbit (1858–1924), the author of several children's books including that perennial favourite *The Railway Children* (1906). She had first discovered this area of Kent in 1893 when she visited Dymchurch, which was then a quiet little fishing village, and she stayed in various holiday homes there during the next few years.

as the gardening correspondent for *The Observer*. To some degree she was right, because today she is best known for her highly influential gardening skills which reached their zenith at Sissinghurst Castle and whose style has spread across the globe.

Vita and her husband, Harold Nicolson, bought Sissinghurst Castle in 1930, when it was little more than a collection of dilapidated buildings surrounded by fields of cabbages, brambles and rusty sardine tins. Despite such an unprepossessing prospect, the Nicolsons were enchanted and began the long process of turning Sissinghurst into a habitable home. It took five years alone before they had mains water and electricity.

Vita and Harold had already created one garden at their previous home, Long Barn in Weald village, but now they set about creating something on a much larger and more ambitious scale. Harold, who was initially a diplomat and later an MP, was also a writer

'Bohemian' is a word that is often applied to Edith Nesbit because of her rather outré life at a time when most of Britain was clutching its collective skirts and avoiding mention of anything improper. Edith, on the other hand, believed in living life to the full. After the death in 1914 of Hubert Bland, her almost compulsively unfaithful first husband, she married Thomas Terry Tucker in February 1917. Edith called him 'the Skipper' as he had once been the captain of the Woolwich Ferry.

They lived in London, but wanted to buy some property around Dymchurch and settled on two huts in the area that was then called Jesson but is now known as St Mary's Bay. The two huts were given suitably nautical names: The Long Boat and The Jolly Boat, and were linked by a passageway called 'the Quarterdeck Gangway'. The kitchen was 'the Galley' and the Skipper would invite their guests to 'come on board'.

They loved their unusual home and when Edith became terminally ill she told the Skipper that she wanted to be buried under an elm tree in the churchyard at St Mary in the Marsh, with no memorial stone to her. The Skipper carved a simple wooden memorial to her, on the back of which is the one word 'Resting', which marks where she was buried in May 1924. In 1958, 100 years after Edith's birth, a stone tablet in her memory was placed inside the church.

Edith Nesbit was not the only writer who lived at St Mary in the Marsh during the 1920s. Noel Coward took a house here with his rather difficult mother, Violet, for a brief spell in 1921. He wrote one of his first and most controversial plays, *The Vortex*, in a converted stable next to The Star Inn. It was during this sojourn that he met Edith Nesbit, whose books he had always loved, and much to his delight they became great friends, although Edith made it plain that she was not nearly so keen on Coward's mother, who immediately labelled her 'stuck-up'.

Romney Marsh used to be a favourite haunt of smugglers, which inspired Russell Thorndike (1885–1972) to write *Dr Syn* (1915) while he was living in a boat-house in Dymchurch. The novel was so successful that Thorndike wrote six more novels about Dr Syn, a Jekyll and Hyde character who is a gentle vicar by day and a smuggler by night. These books were set in the 18th century although there were still smugglers on the

Marsh when the Reverend Richard Barham (1788–1845) was vicar of Snargate and Warehorne from 1813–20. He lived in the rectory next to Warehorne church, and later set many of the stories in *The Ingoldsby Legends* (1840) in Kentish villages.

Canterbury

KENT

In 1170, the Archbishop of Canterbury, Thomas Becket (c. 1118–70), was murdered in Canterbury Cathedral by four knights who believed, mistakenly or otherwise, that they were acting on the orders of King Henry II. The site of Becket's assassination became a place of pilgrimage and by the 14th century it was one of the three most popular shrines in the world. The other two, in Rome and Jerusalem, were

BELOW: Canterbury has literary associations going back to the life of Geoffrey Chaucer, whose bawdy *The Canterbury Tales* recorded the stories of a variety of people making a pilgrimage to the city.

ABOVE: King's School in Canterbury has an illustrious roll call of old boys, which includes Somerset Maugham, Christopher Marlowe and Hugh Walpole.

inaccessible for most inhabitants of Britain who flocked to Canterbury instead.

Geoffrey Chaucer (c. 1343–1400), who was the brother-in-law of John of Gaunt and a member of the royal household, visited Canterbury and was inspired to write *The Canterbury Tales* as a result. He began the book in about 1387, and made it a collection of stories about some of the pilgrims who meet at the Tabard Inn in Southwark before they make the journey to Canterbury.

Becket's murder was the inspiration for T.S. Eliot, who told the story in his poetic drama *Murder in the Cathedral* (1935). It was commissioned for that year's Cathedral Festival and was such a success that it was then performed in London.

Canterbury has had many other literary associations over the centuries. In 1724, Daniel Defoe (1660–1731) preached at Blackfriars church. He was at the height of his creative powers, having already written *Robinson Crusoe* (1719) and *Moll Flanders* (1722). Jane Austen visited the city to see her brother, Edward, and later often stayed at Goodnestone Park outside Canterbury.

Charles Dickens, who lived in Kent for many years, took great pleasure in visiting Canterbury and, in particular, in giving his visitors a special guided tour around the cathedral. Canterbury also appeared in *David Copperfield*. The title character attended Dr Strong's school in the city, and the ever-optimistic Mr Micawber and his family lodged at the Sun Hotel (now a shop) in Sun Street. Dickens knew the hotel well as he used to stay there himself when he visited the city.

Mary Tourtel (1874–1948), the creator of the cartoon character Rupert Bear who delighted generations of children in his yellow scarf and check trousers, trained at the Sidney Cooper School of Art in St Peter's Street. She was buried in 1948 in the churchyard of St Martin's, which is the oldest parish church in England that is still in constant use.

Canterbury is home to one of the oldest schools in Britain, King's School, which stands close to the cathedral. It has an impressive list of old boys, including Somerset Maugham (1874–1965) who may have hated the school when he had to attend it but in later years felt sufficiently generous to endow it with a new library. The Maugham Library contains copies of all his books, as well as the manuscripts of his first and last novels: *Liza of Lambeth* (1897) and *Catalina* (1948) respectively. One of his best-known novels, *Of Human Bondage* (1915), is a *roman à clef* in which the central character, Philip Carey, is Maugham. He has a miserable time at his school in Tercanbury, which is Canterbury in very thin disguise. After Maugham's death in the South of France in 1965, his ashes were buried beneath a rose bush that grows under the window of the library.

The playwright Christopher Marlowe (1564–93) was born in St George's Street in Canterbury in 1564 and christened in St George's Church. Both buildings were bombed during the Second World War and only the tower of the church remains. Marlowe was the son of a cobbler and won a scholarship to King's School. From here, he won another scholarship to Cambridge University, where it is rumoured he was recruited as a spy for Elizabeth I. Marlowe became a poet and playwright, and his most famous works include the poem 'Come Live with Me and be My Love' (1599) and the play *Dr Faustus* (1604), which were both published posthumously. He died in London during a brawl in a tavern in Deptford. The circumstances were mysterious and continue to puzzle historians.

Another old boy, William Somner (1598–1669), wrote the first guide book to Canterbury in 1640. It was the start of the English Civil War and, unfortunately, Somner's book, *Antiquities of Canterbury*, was so

ABOVE: H.G. Wells enjoyed the maritime delights of his home in Sandgate Bay for nine years, during which time he entertained many writers, including Conrad, Shaw, Kipling and Henry James.

BELOW: Joseph Conrad spent the last years of his life near Canterbury. Born Teodor Josef Konrad Korzeniowski to Polish parents in Ukraine in 1857, he became a British subject in 1886.

informative that it helped the Parliamentarians to invade the city. This must have annoyed Somner, who was a Royalist. However, in 1660 he had the pleasure of presenting a copy of his book to Charles II when he landed in Dover.

From 1920 until his death four years later, Joseph Conrad lived at the rectory (now called Oswalds) near Bishopsbourne Church, outside Canterbury. He wrote many books, including *Lord Jim* (1900), *Nostromo* (1904) and the short story, 'Heart of Darkness' (1902), which later became the basis of the film *Apocalypse Now* (1979). In 1924, his funeral mass was held in St Thomas's Church, Canterbury, and he was buried in Canterbury cemetery.

Ian Fleming (1908–64), who made his name as the creator of the James Bond novels, lived for a short time at Bekesbourne near Canterbury, and wrote *You Only Live Twice* (1964) at The Duck, Pett Bottom.

Sandgate Bay

KENT

After a difficult start in life, when he was apprenticed to a draper, an experience he immortalized in his novel *Kipps* (1905), the fate of Herbert George Wells began to improve. He gained a scholarship to the Normal School of Science in London, where he was taught biology by T.H. Huxley (1825– 95), the grandfather of the novelist Aldous (1894–1963). Although Wells left before he was able to take his degree, his enthusiasm for science had been kindled. What seemed like a scholastic failure at the time turned out to be a marvellous preparation for his later career as the author of some of the most notable science-fiction novels of the 20th century.

ABOVE: According to Noël Coward's friends, visiting him in Kent was just like visiting him in London except it was in a rural setting. Even so, he tried to keep chickens at White Cliffs in St Margaret's Bay.

Wells' first novel was *The Time Machine* (1895) and by 1898 he was doing so well that he and his second wife, Catherine, could afford to commission the eminent architect C.F. Voysey (1857–1941) to build Spade House for them in Sandgate Bay near Folkestone. They lived here until 1909 when they returned to London.

At first Wells worked in the study in the house, and then later moved out to a room in the garden. During his time at Sandgate he wrote *Kipps, Tono-Bungay* (1909) and *The History of Mr Polly* (1910). Wells enjoyed a busy social life, which included visiting his friend Henry James at Lamb House (see pages 36–7) in Rye until they fell out over artistic differences. He was also involved in the Fabian Society, which was led by Beatrice and Sidney Webb, with help from George Bernard Shaw.

This trio invited Wells to join the society, but then regretted it when he tried to change it from a debating group for intellectuals to a large pressure group that demanded social reform. Inevitably, Wells' relationship with the Fabians came to a difficult end.

St Margaret's Bay

DOVER, KENT

Noël Coward's love affair with Kent began in the 1920s when he and his mother rented a house at St Mary in the Marsh (see pages 40–41), from where he became part of the rather Bohemian literary set in Rye. Coward (1899–1973) later moved to Goldenhurst Farm near Aldington, which he owned and adored for 30 years. It was requisitioned by the army during the Second World War, but they failed to notify him when they moved out and so he believed that he was without a country retreat.

When his friend, the Hon. Kay Norton, told him she was selling her house at St Margaret's Bay, within sight of the White Cliffs of Dover, Coward leapt at the chance to buy it, even though it had also been requisitioned by the army and left in a bad way. When he finally learned that the army had vacated Goldenhurst Farm, he kept it, even though it was in a terrible condition, and gradually had it renovated.

Coward loved the dramatic position of the St Margaret's Bay house, which, naturally enough, was called White Cliffs, and was thrilled at being able to see and hear the sea from his bedroom. Three other houses stood close to White Cliffs and were empty, so Coward lost no time in filling them with his friends: his secretary-manager, Lorn Lorraine, took one; another was leased to the novelist, Eric Ambler (1909–98), and his wife; and Noël's mother, Violet, and aunt, Vida, were installed in the third.

White Cliffs became one of the lynchpins of Coward's life, from where he entertained a string of famous friends whenever he was in Kent. He was also able to work from here, at his usual hectic pace; his output included *Ace of Clubs, Relative Values, Quadrille* and *Nude with Violin*. However, he found the maritime bustle of White Cliffs too distracting and moved back to his beloved Goldenhurst in the early 1950s.

Ian Fleming took over the lease of White Cliffs. He and his wife, Ann, were tremendous friends of Coward and so the vibrant house parties oscillated between White Cliffs and Goldenhurst. In 1956, Coward reluctantly sold both his London house and Goldenhurst, and moved to Jamaica, in order to escape the high rate of British taxation. He spent the rest of his life on the Caribbean island, in houses that always overlooked the sea, just as White Cliffs had done.

Broadstairs

KENT

The life and works of Charles Dickens are closely connected with Kent; it was the county he moved to when he was five, and many scenes from his books took place in various places there. Dickens was a keen walker and enjoyed striding through the Kent countryside. He particularly liked Broadstairs, and brought his family for at least a month's holiday each summer from 1839 to 1851. Even when he went abroad he had a habit of unfavourably comparing the foreign scenery with Broadstairs, which he always found so much better.

That first summer, in 1839, the family stayed in Albion Street, in buildings that have now become part of the Albion Hotel. A short distance away, in Victoria Parade, is the Dickens House Museum. This contains exhibits in memory of the author, but it has additional interest because it featured strongly in *David Copperfield* (1850). This was the house in which David's aunt, Miss Betsey Trotwood, lived and had so much trouble with the donkeys that used to invade her garden. In the novel, Dickens placed the house in Dover, presumably to protect the privacy of its owner, Miss Mary Pearson Strong.

Dickens had no need to stay in a hotel in Broadstairs after he found Fort House, which is now known as Bleak House. Dickens took great delight in watching the sea from the window of his study there. This was where he finished writing *David Copperfield*, which was his favourite and, in many ways, most autobiographical novel. Dickens was an indefatigable writer, and he often spent eight hours each day working

ABOVE: Charles Dickens had a life-long love of his native county of Kent and took great pleasure in spending his holidays in Broadstairs as an antidote to his working life in London.

on *David Copperfield*; he wrote like a man possessed.

It was in the study of Fort House that Dickens began to plot his next novel, *Bleak House* (1853), after which the house is now named, although the original Bleak House is thought to be in St Albans. The study is also the room in which Dickens wrote an article about Broadstairs in 1851, entitled 'Our English Watering Place'. It is a paean to the many delights of the town but, coupled with Dickens' celebrity, it made Broadstairs such a popular resort that it was no longer the tranquil refuge that Dickens desired, and he had little option but to go elsewhere for his summer holidays. His last visit to Fort House took place in May 1851.

Bleak House is now a museum in which several rooms have been kept as Dickens knew them. The study was later described in Elizabeth Bowen's novel *Eva Trout* (1969).

CHAPTER 3
London

ELIZABETH BARRETT

As Dr Samuel Johnson so famously observed, when you are tired of London you are tired of life. Johnson certainly never grew bored with the city and enjoyed living in Gough Square in the heart of the metropolis. Many writers have spent time in London – some were just passing through, while others made it their home. Some areas of London are associated with particular writers: Hampstead is connected with Keats,

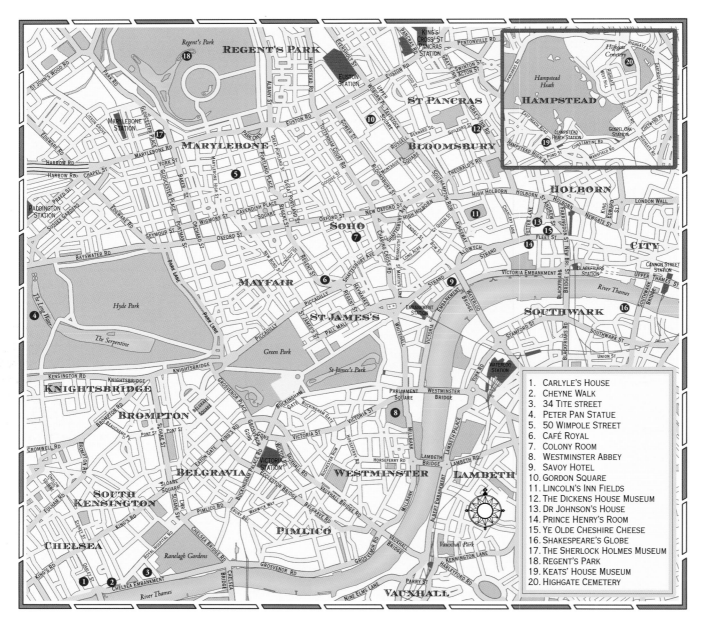

1. CARLYLE'S HOUSE
2. CHEYNE WALK
3. 34 TITE STREET
4. PETER PAN STATUE
5. 50 WIMPOLE STREET
6. CAFÉ ROYAL
7. COLONY ROOM
8. WESTMINSTER ABBEY
9. SAVOY HOTEL
10. GORDON SQUARE
11. LINCOLN'S INN FIELDS
12. THE DICKENS HOUSE MUSEUM
13. DR JOHNSON'S HOUSE
14. PRINCE HENRY'S ROOM
15. YE OLDE CHESHIRE CHEESE
16. SHAKESPEARE'S GLOBE
17. THE SHERLOCK HOLMES MUSEUM
18. REGENT'S PARK
19. KEATS' HOUSE MUSEUM
20. HIGHGATE CEMETERY

JOHN KEATS

even though he spent only a few years there before leaving for Italy in the vain hope of finding a cure for his tuberculosis. Bloomsbury gave its name to the coterie of writers who lived there, including Virginia Woolf and Lytton Strachey. Chelsea is linked with Thomas and Jane Carlyle, who lived modestly in Cheyne Row, and with Oscar Wilde, who lived immodestly in Tite Street. Meanwhile, Baker Street conjures up both Sherlock Holmes and his creator, Sir Arthur Conan Doyle.

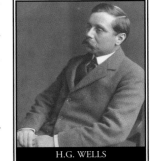

H.G. WELLS

Carlyle's House

24 CHEYNE ROW, SW3

When Thomas Carlyle (1795–1881) and his wife, Jane (1801–66) moved to Cheyne Row from their Scottish farm in Craigenputtock in 1834, they hoped that London life would offer them the culture they craved. They moved into what was then 5 Cheyne Row, although the street has since been renumbered and it is now No. 24. They were tenants, and impoverished ones at that, so were unable to make many changes to the property, although Carlyle did build a soundproof study at the top of the house. Their loss is our gain because the house, which is now owned by the National Trust and open to the public, has retained many of the original features that were present when the Carlyles moved in.

They were apparently a devoted couple, although the later publication of their letters – they were prolific correspondents, both to friends and to each other, and Jane was one of the greatest letter-writers of the Victorian age – revealed the tensions within their marriage. When it was suggested to their friend, the poet Alfred, Lord Tennyson, that perhaps Thomas and Jane should never have married, he commented 'by any other arrangement, four people would have been unhappy instead of two'.

Thomas Carlyle's stature as one of the great men of letters of his day – he became known as 'the sage of Chelsea' – was confirmed by the publication of the *History of the French Revolution* in 1837. This book literally had a baptism of fire because Carlyle lent the original manuscript to his friend, the intellectual John Stuart Mill (1806–73), to read. Mill's maid used the manuscript to light a fire because she wrongly assumed it was a pile of waste paper, and Carlyle had to write the entire book again. The sole remaining scrap of the original manuscript is now on display in the house. Despite this unfortunate incident, Mill continued his friendship with the Carlyles.

The names of other visitors to their house in Cheyne Row reads like a list of the most celebrated writers of the day and includes John Ruskin (1819–1900); Tennyson; Charles Dickens; Dickens's biographer John Forster (1812–76); Robert Browning (1812–89); George Eliot; and J.A. Froude (1818–94). Froude caused major controversy when he published his *Reminiscences* of Thomas in 1881 and the *Letters and Memorials* of Jane in 1883, as both volumes were so frank about their subjects' characters.

LEFT: George Eliot had a very short tenancy of 4 Cheyne Walk as she died only three weeks after moving in. Her unconventional life was a source of moral outrage for Victorian Britain.

PREVIOUS PAGE: Many of Charles Dickens's possessions are now on display at The Dickens House Museum, 48 Doughty Street, WC1.

Jane died suddenly of a heart attack in 1866 while taking a carriage ride around Hyde Park. Carlyle wrote that her death 'shattered my whole existence into immeasurable ruin', and started to retreat from the world. After Carlyle died in 1881 the house was occupied for a short time by a tenant whose many pets roamed freely through the rooms and over the furniture. However, this caused such an outcry among Thomas and Jane's many admirers that the house was bought by a committee in 1895, before being restored and opened to the public.

Cheyne Walk

SW3, SW10

Cheyne Walk has long been one of London's greatest literary streets and it has been familiar to many writers since the 19th century, whether they were visiting friends or lived here themselves. Many of the houses date from the reign of Queen Anne (1702–14) and have interesting architectural features.

In 1862, Dante Gabriel Rossetti rented No. 16. He was not an ideal neighbour as he kept a small menagerie, which included peacocks that screeched so loudly that later tenants were legally banned from keeping them. Rossetti stayed here until 1882, during which time the house was the meeting place of many artists and poets. Algernon Swinburne (1837–1909) stayed here from time to time, writing poetry in the first-floor drawing room; and George Meredith (1828–1909), who lived round the corner at 8 Hobury Street from 1858–59, Oscar Wilde and William Morris were also frequent visitors to the house.

A drinking fountain in memory of Rossetti stands between Cheyne Walk and the Embankment, with a bronze medallion of the poet cast by his friend and fellow Pre-Raphaelite, Ford Madox Brown (1821–93), in 1887.

George Eliot moved into 4 Cheyne Walk in early December 1880 with her new husband, John Cross. Neither of them was well but no one realized quite how ill Eliot was, and she died of renal failure in the house on 22 December the same year. She was 61, and her life had been a turbulent mixture of great critical acclaim and scandal.

The novelist Henry James spent each winter from 1912 at Carlyle Mansions, on the corner of Lawrence Street, and died here in 1916. There is a memorial plaque to him in the churchyard of Chelsea Old Church, which is on the corner of Old Church Street.

Elizabeth Stevenson, who later became known as Mrs Gaskell (1810–65), the author of a number of novels including *Wives and Daughters* (1866), was born at 93 Cheyne Walk. She spent the first year of her life here until she was taken to Knutsford, Cheshire, which she immortalized in *Cranford* (1853). Hilaire Belloc (1870–1953) and his wife lived at No. 104 from 1901 to 1905, at the start of his writing career. Belloc's classic book of children's verse, *Cautionary Tales*, was published in 1907.

34 Tite Street

SW3

This was the home of Oscar Wilde (1854–1900) from 1885 until his imprisonment in 1895. He already knew the street, having lived at No. 1 for a short time in 1880 with his fellow Oxford graduate, Frank Miles. Wilde called No. 1 'Keats House', although this was a joke because the house had nothing to do with the poet.

Wilde moved back to Tite Street on 1 January 1885 with his wife, Constance, whom he had married in May 1884. Constance was pregnant and the couple's elder son, Cyril, was born at home in June 1885. Their younger son, Vyvyan, was born in November 1886. In their day, their house was 16 Tite Street although it is now No. 34. In order to support his new

LEFT: Oscar Wilde cultivated his aesthetic image and believed in 'Art for art's sake'.

family, Wilde became editor of *The Woman's World* magazine from 1887 to 1889. He also wrote his most noted plays and books while living here, including *The Happy Prince* (1888), *The Picture of Dorian Gray* (1891), *Lady Windermere's Fan* (1892), *A Woman of No Importance* (1893), *An Ideal Husband* (1895) and *The Importance of Being Earnest* (1895).

In 1891, trouble arrived for Wilde in the shape of Lord Alfred 'Bosie' Douglas (1870–1945), who was the third son of the Marquess of Queensberry. Wilde was no stranger to intense relationships with men, and he and Bosie soon became lovers. Unfortunately, Bosie's father got wind of what was happening and sent Wilde what he considered to be a libellous note about his homosexuality. Wilde duly sued Queensberry for libel before withdrawing the action, but by then Queensberry had dredged up so much incriminating evidence against Wilde that he was tried for homosexuality, which was then illegal, and imprisoned for two years with hard labour. His sentence began at Wandsworth Prison and he was later transferred to Reading, about which he wrote *The Ballad of Reading Gaol* (1898).

BELOW: Oscar Wilde lived at 34 Tite Street with his wife and their two sons until scandal broke in 1895 when he was imprisoned for homosexuality. It was the beginning of the end for him.

All of Wilde's belongings were removed from Tite Street and sold the day before the first trial came to court. Constance took her two sons to live in Switzerland, where they changed their name to Holland, which had family connections for her. She died in 1898 and Wilde died two years later, broken and bankrupt, having lived in France for the final years of his life. But Wilde's wit had not deserted him, and even when he lay dying in a Paris hotel room he told his old friend and supporter, Robert Ross, that he was 'dying beyond my means'. He died in November 1900 and, after a temporary burial at Bagneux, his body was moved to Père Lachaise cemetery in Paris in 1909.

Peter Pan Statue

KENSINGTON GARDENS, W8

*P*eter Pan, the play about the boy who never grew up, was first performed in 1904. It was written by J.M. Barrie (1860–1937), who based it on the stories he used to tell the five boys whose guardian he became after the death of their parents, Arthur and Sylvia Llewellyn Davies. His charges inspired the Lost Boys in the play, whose leader was Peter Pan.

Barrie was already a well-known playwright, but the success of *Peter Pan* made him famous. He followed it with *Peter and Wendy*, which was a novelization of the play, in 1911.

Barrie lived in Bayswater Road between 1902 and 1909, and often took his dog, Luath (who became Nana in the play), for a walk in Kensington Gardens. It was here that he first met the Llewellyn Davies boys, so the gardens had strong sentimental associations for him. In 1912, Barrie paid for a bronze statue of Peter Pan, surrounded by fairies and animals, to be erected on the west bank of the Long Water, which is part of the Serpentine. The statue was erected in secret one night, and has delighted generations of children ever since.

50 Wimpole Street

W1

The story of Elizabeth Barrett and Robert Browning is one of the great literary romances. It began in January 1845 when Robert wrote a fan letter to Elizabeth. She was by this time the celebrated author of *The Seraphim, and Other Poems* (1838) and *Poems* (1844), but Robert was also making a name for himself, especially after the publication of *Paracelsus* in 1835. Elizabeth admired his work and was delighted to make his epistolary acquaintance. He was the kindred spirit she had been searching for.

They met for the first time in May 1845. Elizabeth was an invalid who suffered from recurrent chest complaints, which may have been tuberculosis, so she had to receive Browning lying on her sofa in the back room at 50 Wimpole Street. Despite her wan appearance, which was not improved by the black she still wore in mourning for her brother, Bro, who had drowned in 1840 (see pages 15–16), Browning fell in love with her and wrote asking her to marry him. Elizabeth was aghast, perhaps even terrified, telling him that he must not mention such things again if he wished to continue to see her. She had good reason to be wary, as her deeply religious father had convinced himself that the Bible backed up his belief that none of his 12 children should ever marry.

The friendship continued and blossomed into love, although Elizabeth was insistent that her father should not know about this change in her relationship with Browning. She cast her father as an ogre, who would rather see her 'dead at his foot' than married. Eventually, the couple decided that the only option

ABOVE: The bronze statue of Peter Pan in Kensington Gardens was erected in secret one night in 1912, at the behest of J.M. Barrie, ready to be discovered by excited children the following morning.

was to marry in secret and then elope a short time later. They married on 12 September 1846 and then went their separate ways immediately afterwards. A week later, they left London – Elizabeth crept out of Wimpole Street while the rest of the family was sitting down to dinner. She had already posted farewell letters to her family, which arrived the next day.

Elizabeth and Browning spent their honeymoon in Paris and then moved on to Italy where they lived in Florence for the rest of their married life. Elizabeth gave birth to their son, Robert, whom they nicknamed 'Pen', in March 1849 when she was 43. She died in Florence in June 1861 and was buried in the Protestant cemetery there. Browning and Pen returned to London, where Browning lived at 19 Warwick Crescent until 1889, when he died at his son's house in Venice.

ABOVE: The Café Royal, with its lavishly decorated interior, appeared in the novels of many writers, including Evelyn Waugh, Arnold Bennett and Somerset Maugham.

Café Royal

68 REGENT STREET, W1

After the Café Royal was built by the French wine merchant, Daniel Nicols, in 1885 it became a great haunt of many artists and writers. It was also a favourite watering hole of members of the Aesthetic Movement, who prided themselves on their effete clothing and exaggerated style of conversation. One of the greatest exponents of the movement was Oscar Wilde, for whom the Café Royal became the stage set for some of the most dramatic moments in his life.

In the summer of 1891, Wilde met an Adonis-like young man called Lord Alfred Douglas, whom he called 'Bosie'. They became lovers, although such a relationship could not be spoken about in polite Victorian society; it was, in the words of one of Bosie's poems, 'the love that dare not speak its name'. In the autumn of 1892, Bosie's father, the Marquess of Queensberry, became concerned about the nature of his son's relationship with the older playwright, so Wilde invited him to lunch at the Café Royal in order to put his mind at rest. Wilde spared no expense in winning over the irascible marquess, and it seemed to do the trick for the time being. However, by February 1895, Queensberry confronted Wilde with the truth, and Wilde sued for libel.

Wilde hosted another lunch at the Café Royal, at which he discussed the situation with Bosie and two friends and fellow Irishmen, George Bernard Shaw, and Frank Harris (1856–1931), who was the louche editor of the *Saturday Review*. Shaw and Harris tried to persuade Wilde to drop the case and go to live in France, which had a more tolerant attitude to homosexuality. But Bosie and Wilde disagreed and the case came to court. It ended in disaster for Wilde. He was arrested on a charge of gross indecency, and tracked down at the Cadogan Hotel in Sloane Street, where he was having a crisis meeting with Douglas and Robert Ross. Wilde's name was almost immediately removed from the playbills at the St James Theatre, where *The Importance of Being Earnest* was being performed.

Wilde was not the only literary figure to enjoy the Café Royal, although he was certainly one of the most notorious. Another customer who attracted notoriety was the occultist Aleister Crowley (1875–1947), who frequented the Café Royal with his friend, Arnold Bennett (1867–1931). Aubrey Beardsley (1872–98), Max Beerbohm (1872–1956), H.G. Wells and his lover, Rebecca West (1892–1983), were also regular customers.

Colony Room

41 DEAN STREET, W1

On 15 December 1948, a young woman called Muriel Belcher opened a club on the first floor of 41 Dean Street in the heart of Soho. There were few customers at first, although the Colony Room later became a Mecca for many of the writers and artists for whom Soho was a spiritual home. At the time, in the late 1940s and early 1950s, Soho was a grimy, gritty place where gangsters rubbed shoulders with impoverished artists, such as Francis Bacon (1909–92) and Lucian Freud (born 1922), and with writers, such as Keith Waterhouse (born 1929), Dan Farson (1927–97) and Dylan Thomas (1914–53).

Muriel Belcher was renowned, and in some circles notorious, for her filthy language and extreme rudeness. One customer whose rudeness was equal to hers was Colin MacInnes (1914–76), the author of *City of Spades* (1957) and *Absolute Beginners* (1959). Both books championed the black cause long before it became fashionable. MacInnes, who delighted in being a member of rackety Soho, was profoundly embarrassed by his mother, who was the novelist, Angela Thirkell (1890–1961). He described her as 'an immensely successful and bad writer'.

It was difficult to get into the Colony Room because Muriel Belcher was very careful to weed out the people she considered boring. However, theatregoers who were unable to visit the club in person could visit it vicariously after Rodney Ackland wrote the play *Absolute Hell* (1987), where the action took place in a club named La Vie en Rose, which was obviously the Colony. In the play it was presided over by a woman, Christine Foskett, who was clearly based on Muriel Belcher. The play, which was well received, was a reworking of his earlier play, *The Pink Room* (1952), which had received a savage roasting by the critics of the day.

Westminster Abbey

SW1

Just about anyone who is anyone is buried in Westminster Abbey. It is the resting place of many kings and queens, politicians, soldiers and campaigners. Indeed, the north aisle is so heavily populated with monuments to politicians that it is sometimes known as Statesman's Aisle. Another concentration of memorials can be found in the south transept, in an area that is now known as Poets' Corner.

Geoffrey Chaucer was the first poet to be buried here in 1400, but that was purely because he had been Clerk of Works to the Palace of Westminster and therefore deserved a decent resting place. However, by the 16th century, Chaucer was revered as the author of *The Canterbury Tales*, and so he was given a more prestigious tomb. Edmund Spenser (c. 1552–99), the Elizabethan poet and courtier and author of *The Faerie Queen* (1590), died in 1599 and was buried near Chaucer, thereby unwittingly instigating a tradition that has continued ever since.

Literary celebrity has never been an automatic passport to commemoration in Poets' Corner. This is, after all, a sacred burial place and not every poet or writer has been considered to have lived a life worthy of such a posthumous honour. George Eliot, who outraged Victorian society by living openly with her married lover, G.H. Lewes (1817–78), and writing under a masculine pseudonym instead of her real name of Mary Ann Evans, was excluded from Poets' Corner after her death and buried in Highgate Cemetery instead. Nevertheless, a memorial stone was placed in Poets' Corner in 1980 to mark the centenary of her death. Charles Dickens, on the other hand, did not lead a blameless life but, when he died in 1870, his great celebrity meant that the public insisted on him being buried in Poets' Corner – even though he would have preferred the churchyard at Rochester where his family had already secured a place for him.

Other writers who are buried in Poets' Corner include John Dryden, Dr Johnson, Richard Brinsley Sheridan, Tennyson, Robert Browning, John Masefield, Thomas Hardy and Rudyard Kipling. Some are buried elsewhere and only have memorials here,

ABOVE: H.G. Wells used to enjoy visiting the Café Royal with his mistress, Rebecca West.

ABOVE: To be buried in Westminster Abbey is a great honour and one which many of Britain's greatest literary figures have received, from Dryden to Kipling.

including William Shakespeare – who was not given a memorial until 1740 – John Milton, all three of the Brontë sisters, Oliver Goldsmith, John Ruskin, Samuel Butler, Robert Burns, Thomas Gray, William Wordsworth, Percy Bysshe Shelley – whose scandalous life meant that he was only given a memorial in 1969 despite having died in 1824 – Sir Walter Scott, William Blake, Henry James, T.S. Eliot, Gerard Manley Hopkins and Sir John Betjeman.

Savoy Hotel

SAVOY HILL, STRAND, WC2

'My bill here is 49 pounds for a week. I have also got a new sitting-room over the Thames.' So wrote Oscar Wilde to Lord Alfred Douglas in March 1893, while their romance was at its height and before the full weight of outraged Victorian morality descended on Wilde's head (see pages 49–50). During Wilde's subsequent trial in 1895, witnesses were called who testified that he had taken them to his second-floor sitting room at the Savoy for drinks, and later to his bedroom for sex.

Even then the Savoy Hotel was a byword for luxury, and this connection was emphasized by its name, which referred to the old Savoy Palace that had once stood on this spot. The luxurious nature of the hotel made a huge impression on Arnold Bennett when he was taken here for tea at the turn of the 20th century, and inspired him to write *The Grand Babylon Hotel* (1902), which was patently about the Savoy. Bennett was always fascinated by large organizations and the machinations that went on in them, and for many years he delighted in discovering what went on behind the scenes at the Savoy. He had privileged access because by now he was a director of the hotel. In 1927, Bennett was given a guided tour of the labyrinthine service departments that ensure the smooth running of the Savoy, and the knowledge that he gained was invaluable when he came to write *Imperial Palace* (1930), which was also a thinly disguised Savoy.

This literary connection is still remembered at the Savoy. The dish 'Omelette Arnold Bennett', which is made with smoked haddock and parmesan cheese, was named for the novelist and continues to appear on the menu.

Gordon Square

WC1

In the 1920s, Gordon Square was the nerve centre of the literary and artistic set that became known as the Bloomsbury Group after the area of London in which they lived. They were reviled in some circles as jokes and fakes, and adored in others as being at the vanguard of the latest artistic movement. The epicentre round which they revolved was 46 Gordon Square, the home of the children of Sir Leslie Stephen who was the first editor of the *Dictionary of National Biography*. Thoby, Adrian, Virginia and Vanessa Stephen grew up at 22 Hyde Park Gate, but moved to Gordon Square after their father's death in 1904. They began what turned into a ritual of entertaining their friends on Thursday evenings, and soon their rooms were full of such people as Leonard Woolf, Clive Bell and Lytton Strachey. After Thoby died from typhoid in 1906, Vanessa decided to marry Clive Bell, which meant that Virginia and Adrian had to look for a new home. They found it at 29 Fitzroy Square.

Lytton Strachey, who was one of the central figures of the Bloomsbury Group until his death from stomach cancer in 1932, moved to 51 Gordon Square with his family in 1909 and stayed here until 1917. He became a noted essayist, and is perhaps most famous for his books *Eminent Victorians* (1918) and *Queen Victoria* (1921).

Lincoln's Inn Fields

WC2

This square was laid out by Inigo Jones (1573–1652) in 1618 and lies close to Lincoln's Inn, which is one of the four Inns of Court. John Forster, who became the hagiographer of his great friend, Charles Dickens – he omitted all the controversial episodes in Dickens's life– had chambers at No. 58. Forster's house became the home of Mr Tulkinghorn, the Dedlock's family lawyer who comes to a sticky end, in *Bleak House* (1853). Forster also wrote biographies of Walter Savage Landor (1775–1864) and Oliver Goldsmith (*c.* 1730–74), and is believed to be the model for Mr Podsnap in *Our Mutual Friend* (1865). This cannot have been an entirely flattering thought for Forster, as Podsnap 'was well to do, and stood very high in Mr Podsnap's opinion'.

Dickens knew this area well. When he was 14, he spent a short time in Lincoln's Inn as a solicitor's clerk in New Square. No experience was ever wasted for Dickens, and he later used his memories of Lincoln's Inn for several of his novels. In *The Posthumous Papers of the Pickwick Club* (1837), Mr Pickwick visits his leading counsel, Serjeant Snubbin, here when he is being sued for breach of promise by his landlady, Mrs Bardell.

When Dickens wrote *Bleak House*, the Court of Chancery met at Lincoln's Inn, so it became the setting for the case of Jarndyce versus Jarndyce around which the book revolves. The offices of the solicitors, Kenge and Carboy, who are employed by Mr Jarndyce, are in Old Square. Krook's Rag and Bottle Warehouse, where Krook apparently became a case of spontaneous combustion, is in Chichester Rents, near New Square.

Lincoln's Inn was established in the 14th century and was a thriving community of lawyers by the time Samuel Pepys mentioned the gardens in his diaries. John Donne entered the Inn in 1592, and shared rooms with a fellow poet, Christopher Brooke. Donne later became the first Chaplain of the Inn's chapel. Other literary members of the

ABOVE: The home of Virginia, Vanessa, Thoby and Adrian Stephen at 46 Gordon Square was the unofficial headquarters of the Bloomsbury Group. Lytton Strachey later lived at No. 51.
BELOW: Lincoln's Inn Fields is one of the four Inns of Court in London; Temple is another, where John Mortimer and his creation, the indefatigable Horace Rumpole, were barristers.

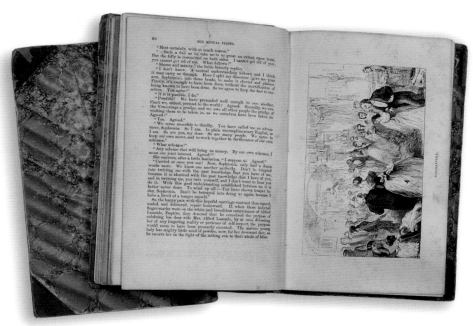

Inn include Lord Macaulay (1800–59), who is best known for his lengthy and detailed *History of England* (1849–55); Thomas Hughes (1822–96), who wrote *Tom Brown's Schooldays* (1857); H. Rider Haggard (1856–1925), author of *King Solomon's Mines* (1886) and *She* (1887); and John Galsworthy (1867–1933), who was called to the Bar in 1890 but swiftly turned to literature and is best known for *The Forsyte Saga* (1922).

The Dickens House Museum

48 DOUGHTY STREET, WC1

ABOVE: Charles Dickens is believed to have based the conceited character of Mr Podsnap from *Our Mutual Friend* on his own friend and later biographer, John Forster.
BELOW: The attic of this elegant house in Gough Square was a hive of industry while Dr Johnson worked on his dictionary. This mammoth work increased his fame but not his finances.

The Dickens family came up in the world when they moved to 48 Doughty Street in the spring of 1837. Their previous home had been a few rooms at 15 Furnival's Inn, but now they could afford a prosperous middle-class road, which was closed off at each end and attended by porters wearing mulberry livery. The household consisted of Charles Dickens; his wife, Catherine; Charles, their baby son; and Dickens's younger brother, Fred. Catherine's sister, Mary Hogarth, was a frequent guest.

In 1837, Dickens's star was on the rise. *The Posthumous Papers of the Pickwick Club* had been running as a serial for a year and was starting to make his name. However, very soon after the family moved to Doughty Street their happiness was shattered by the sudden death of 17-year-old Mary Hogarth. Dickens was so bereft that he had to stop work on *Pickwick Papers* and *Oliver Twist* (1838), which had just begun to appear in monthly instalments. He later used the experience of Mary's death when writing about the demise of Little Nell in *The Old Curiosity Shop* (1841).

Dickens named his eldest daughter, who was born in Doughty Street in March 1838, after his deceased sister-in-law. His second daughter, Kate, was born here in October 1839. Two months later, the Dickens family moved from Doughty Street to 1 Devonshire Terrace in Regent's Park.

Dickens was always a prolific writer, even later in life when his prodigious output damaged his health. During his tenure at Doughty Street, he wrote the last five monthly instalments of *Pickwick Papers*, all of *Oliver Twist* except the first five instalments, the whole of *Nicholas Nickleby* (1839), the first few pages of *Barnaby Rudge* (1841) and several shorter pieces. The house in Doughty Street is now a museum dedicated to Dickens and contains many of his possessions.

Dr Johnson's House

17 GOUGH SQUARE, EC4

In 1746, Dr Samuel Johnson agreed to write what would be the first dictionary of the English language. He outlined his intentions in 1747, which were 'to produce a dictionary by which the pronunciation of our language may be fixed, and its attainment facilitated; by which its purity may be preserved, its use ascertained, and its duration lengthened.' This was no idle boast, and Johnson laboured on the dictionary for nine years, with the help of six assistants. It was published in 1755 to great acclaim and earned him an honorary Oxford degree.

Johnson was paid an advance of £1,575 for compiling the dictionary, and used the money to rent this house in Gough Square. It was the first time he had known any sort of financial security, although it did not last and throughout his life he had periods in which he struggled to make ends meet. When his mother died he could not pay for her funeral, so in order to raise the required funds he dashed off his novel *Rasselas* (1759), which discussed 'the choice of life', in less than a week.

Johnson and his helpers worked on the dictionary in the attic at Gough Square, which is now open to the public. He lived here from 1749 to 1759, and the house is the only one of his London homes to have survived. It contains portraits of Johnson and his contemporaries, as well as a first edition of the dictionary.

Prince Henry's Room

17 FLEET STREET, EC4

Prince Henry's Room is on the first floor of a Jacobean house in Fleet Street and is dedicated to the life and work of Samuel Pepys. It is one of the ironies of Pepys's life that the one book he deliberately wrote for publication, *Memoires Relating to the State of the Royal Navy in England* (1690), sank into obscurity, while his diaries, which he wrote purely for pleasure, continue to be in print over 300 years after he wrote them.

Pepys was born in February 1633 in a court off Fleet Street, and was educated at St Paul's School in the City,

Claret is the liquor for boys; port for men; but he who aspires to be a hero must drink brandy.

DR SAMUEL JOHNSON

and then at Magdalene College, Cambridge (see pages 66–7). When he began writing his diary in 1660 he was working at the Navy Office in London and living in Seething Lane with his wife, Elizabeth. He wrote his diary in a mixture of shorthand and longhand, and although it was not exactly a secret from his wife he did not advertise its existence either. Pepys recorded every detail of his life, from what he ate to his rows with his wife, and also vividly described what turned out to be a very eventful decade in London's history, with the restoration of Charles II to the throne in 1660, the Great Plague in 1665 and the Great Fire in 1666. He only stopped writing his diary, in 1669, because he wrongly feared that he was going blind.

ABOVE: Ye Olde Cheshire Cheese has been a Fleet Street institution for centuries, and was a particular favourite with Oliver Goldsmith who lived round the corner in the 18th century.

and Johnson first met in 1761, and Goldsmith became one of the founding members of Johnson's literary group, which was called 'The Club'.

The youthful Charles Dickens used to walk up and down Fleet Street, pressing his nose to the windows of food shops in the vain hope that the sight of food would somehow satisfy his empty stomach. Once he began to earn money, he used to drink in Ye Olde Cheshire Cheese, and undoubtedly enjoyed soaking up the historic atmosphere too. His portrait, as well as those of Johnson and Goldsmith, hangs on the wall, and there is a plaque in his memory. One of the establishment's most famous traditions was to serve an extremely hefty pudding on the first Monday of October; apparently Dickens liked to be the person to make the first incision into these culinary whoppers before they were served to all the diners.

In 1891, the pub became the headquarters of a group of poets calling themselves the Rhymers' Club. They met here for a couple of years to read their poetry, and they included W.B. Yeats (1865–1939) and Arthur Symons (1865–1945), who was known for poems that celebrated the *demi-monde* that was so fashionable at the time.

Ye Olde Cheshire Cheese

WINE OFFICE COURT, EC4

This pub, which is situated just off Fleet Street, can rightly claim to be 'olde', as the sign that hangs outside it acknowledges that it was 'rebuilt in 1667'. It was here that Dr Samuel Johnson retreated whenever his work on his monumental *Dictionary* (1775) and his later books got too much for him. Johnson once made the heartfelt statement that 'there is nothing which has yet been contrived by man by which so much happiness is produced as by a good tavern or inn'.

Another writer who enjoyed relaxing in Ye Olde Cheshire Cheese was Oliver Goldsmith, whose lodgings were conveniently placed in Wine Office Court while he was writing *The Vicar of Wakefield* (1766). Goldsmith

Shakespeare's Globe

NEW GLOBE WALK, SE1

In 1989, workmen began digging the foundations for the new Globe Theatre at Bankside. The original, which was built by the brothers Cuthbert and Richard Burbage in 1598–9, had once stood 200 yards away but it was destroyed in 1644 during the English Civil War and all traces of it had long since vanished.

Until, that is, the theatre director, Sam Wanamaker (1919–93), conceived the notion in 1949 that he would like to find it again. It was a project that occupied him, off and on, for the rest of his life and which ended with the triumphant creation of Shakespeare's Globe Theatre.

The new Globe Theatre is as close to the original in appearance as possible, the only differences being those required by modern safety laws. Like the original Globe, the theatre has a thatched roof – the first such roof to exist in central London since the Great Fire of London in 1666 – while the yard at the front of the stage is open to the elements.

The new theatre also performs Shakespeare's plays, just as the old one did. A complete list of the plays performed at the original Globe does not exist, but it is known that the following were definitely staged here: *Love's Labours Lost*, *The Taming of the Shrew*, *King Lear*, *Macbeth*, *Pericles*, *Othello*, *Romeo and Juliet*, *Henry VIII* and *The Winter's Tale*. Shakespeare was a shareholder of the Globe as well as an actor in his plays. He belonged to a troupe of players known as the Lord Chamberlain's Men, which was the biggest theatre company in London at that time. They moved to the Globe after it was completed in 1599 and then, with great political foresight, changed their name to the King's Men in 1603 when James I succeeded to the throne. They could only act at the Globe in the summer, because of its open roof, and from 1608 they began to play winter seasons at the nearby Blackfriars Theatre.

During a performance of *Henry VIII* in 1613, two cannons were fired as usual but a spark from one of them flew up and set the Globe's thatch alight. The theatre burned to the ground, but was rebuilt with the help of public subscriptions and was back in business the following year.

ABOVE: Shakespeare's Globe Theatre is a reconstruction of the original Globe Theatre in which Shakespeare's plays were performed by the man himself and his fellow actors.

The Sherlock Holmes Museum

239 BAKER STREET, NW1

Any Sherlock Holmes fan who is looking for 221B Baker Street, where Sherlock Holmes lived and was looked after by his faithful housekeeper, Mrs Hudson, will imagine that they have found it when they see the sign on the door at this address. Actually, this building is really No. 239, and calling it 221B simply sets the scene for the visitor. The real 221 Baker Street is the home of the Abbey bank, which kindly replies to all the letters it receives addressed to Sherlock Holmes and asking for his help in solving mysteries.

What these correspondents have often forgotten is that Sherlock Holmes is a fictional detective who was created by Sir Arthur Conan Doyle. The first Holmes novel, *A Study in Scarlet*, was published in 1887 and was followed by several short stories that appeared in *The Strand Magazine*. Doyle's second Holmes novel, *The Sign of Four* (1890), featured the luxurious Langham Hotel, where Doyle had dined with Oscar Wilde and an American literary agent.

Doyle lived in Montagu Place, W1, in 1890 and was trying to practise as an oculist at 2 Devonshire Place, but this proved impossible as he could not attract any patients. Never one to waste time, he spent each day writing; a practice that quickly brought him more money and fame than he could ever have received if he had stayed in the medical profession. He swiftly became a full-time writer and wrote many books on a variety of topics, including fairies and spiritualism. He wrote of his experiences in *Memories and Adventures* (1930).

Regent's Park

NW1

To the visitor, London can feel like one giant, sprawling city but, as anyone who has lived here knows, it is really a collection of villages. They all have a distinctive flavour and Regent's Park is no exception. It has a different atmosphere to Hampstead, which is to the north of the park and prides itself on the intelligentsia who live there, but has nevertheless attracted several writers during the years.

H.G. Wells spent the last few years of his life at 13 Hanover Terrace, from 1937 until his death here in 1946. It was while living here that he wrote his last book, *Mind at the End of its Tether* (1945), which expressed his despair at the prospect of another world war. From 1850 to 1859, Wilkie Collins (1824–89) lived a couple of doors away at No. 17 with his mother and brother. It was during this interlude that he began to write for Charles Dickens's *Household Words*, and started his thriller *The Woman in White* (1860). Edmund Gosse (1849–1928), the poet and biographer, lived in the same house from 1901 to 1928. While he was here he wrote *Father and Son* (1907), which records his very difficult relationship with his fundamentalist father.

Elizabeth Bowen (1899–1973), who was born in Dublin, lived at 2 Clarence Terrace from 1935 to 1952 with her husband, Alan Campbell. She wrote several novels while she was here, including *The Death of the Heart* (1938). She was an air-raid warden during the war, and the experience inspired many of her short stories.

Primrose Hill lies to the east of Regent's Park and has also had some literary residents. These include W.B. Yeats, who lived with his family at 23 Fitzroy Road from 1867 to 1874; his residency is commemorated by a plaque. This is the same house where the poet Sylvia Plath (1932–63) committed suicide. She had previously lived in a flat at 3 Chalcot Square with her husband and fellow poet, Ted Hughes (1930–98). The author Kingsley Amis (1922–95) also lived in Primrose Hill, in Regent's Park Road, and used to drink in the Queen's pub.

Keats' House Museum

10 KEATS GROVE, NW3

In 1818, John Keats (1795–1821) was just beginning his career as a poet. He had abandoned his training as an apothecary in 1816 so he could concentrate on poetry instead, and his first volume of poems was published in 1817. His work had its detractors, chiefly in the writer John Lockhart (1794–1854) who wrote some scathing attacks on Keats and claimed he belonged to the 'Cockney School of Poetry'.

During this period, Keats went to live with his friend, Charles Armitage Brown (1786–1842), in Hampstead. The semi-detached house was called Wentworth Place; the two houses were converted into one building in the 1830s and later renamed Keats' House. The Brawne family lived next door and Keats soon fell in love with the young daughter, Fanny. Both personally and artistically, the following two years were the greatest of Keats' life. He wrote many of his most enduring and best-loved poems, including 'The Eve of St Agnes', 'Ode to a Nightingale', which it is claimed he wrote after sitting under a plum tree in the front garden of the house, and 'Ode on a Grecian Urn'.

BELOW: Although John Keats only lived in Keats' House for two years, he wrote many of his finest poems here. He left for Italy in 1820 after developing the first symptoms of tuberculosis.

Keats and Fanny became engaged, but the young poet soon realized that he was becoming ill with tuberculosis, which had already killed his brother, Tom. After Keats first coughed up blood in the four-poster bed that is on display in Keats' House, he told his friend, Charles, 'that drop of blood is my death warrant'. The only solution was for Keats to leave the damp, sooty air of England and go to Italy in the hope that the warmer climate would cure him, but he died in Rome in February 1821, at the age of 25.

Wentworth Place continued to be a private home until plans arose to demolish it to make way for new buildings. However, the house was bought by public subscription and the newly named Keats' House was first opened as a museum in May 1925.

Highgate Cemetery

N6

This is one of the greatest 'garden' cemeteries in England, although in fact it consists of two cemeteries that lie on either side of Swains Lane: the West Cemetery, which opened in 1839, and the East Cemetery, which opened in 1854.

This was where many members of the great, the good and sometimes the not-so-good were buried, and it was highly sought-after as the final resting place of wealthy Victorians. However, its fortunes dwindled when its plots filled up and parts of it are now highly atmospheric examples of Victorian sentimentality at its best.

Many Victorian authors who achieved fame were either buried in Westminster Abbey (see pages 53–4) if the Dean approved, or were buried in Highgate Cemetery if they were either refused permission to enter those hallowed grounds or had no wish to do so. George Eliot, the female novelist whose life was considered outrageous, was buried in the East Cemetery in 1880. Her married lover, the writer G.H. Lewes, had been buried in the cemetery two years before. Sir Leslie Stephen, who was another Victorian man of letters and the father of Vanessa Bell and Virginia Woolf, was buried in the East Cemetery in 1904.

The death of a loved one sometimes brings out the worst in their survivors, so it is hardly surprising that there are controversies connected with Highgate Cemetery. When Elizabeth Siddall, who was the wife of Dante Gabriel Rossetti and the favourite model of the Pre-Raphaelite painters, committed suicide in 1862 she was buried in the Rossetti family vault in the West Cemetery. Distraught with remorse at the way he had

ABOVE: Highgate Cemetery is the final resting place of many literary figures, including Douglas Adams, author of *The Hitch-hiker's Guide to the Galaxy*, whose ashes were interred here in 2001.

treated her, her husband buried the only manuscript of his love poems with her. Seven years later, however, times were hard for Rossetti and he began to think longingly of those buried poems and the money they could earn him, so he arranged to have his wife's coffin exhumed. It appears that when her coffin was opened, Rossetti was shocked to discover that her long auburn hair had continued to grow after her death. Rossetti's sister, the poet Christina (1830–94), was also buried in the family tomb, but was allowed to rest there undisturbed. The mournful setting matches the mood of some of her more melancholy poetry.

Other literary figures who were buried here include Frederick Warne, who was Beatrix Potter's publisher; Mrs Henry Wood (1814–87), whose first novel *East Lynne* (1861) was such a success; novelist Stella Gibbons (1902–89), who is chiefly remembered for her first novel, *Cold Comfort Farm* (1932); and Radclyffe Hall, the author of *The Well of Loneliness* (1928).

CHAPTER 4

East Anglia

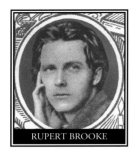

RUPERT BROOKE

The flat fenland counties of East Anglia have a particular atmosphere that comes through very strongly in the books that have links with this part of England. They have a mysterious quality that may explain why so many crime and thriller writers have been attracted to the region. Many classic detective novelists have lived in and written about East Anglia, including Margery Allingham, Dorothy L. Sayers and P.D. James. Dick Francis got to know Newmarket during his career as a jockey, and then created an even more successful career by writing many thrillers connected with horse-racing, which is romantically known as 'the sport of kings'. The city of Cambridge offers another aspect of East Anglia, with its beautiful old colleges and associations over the centuries with many important writers, poets and novelists.

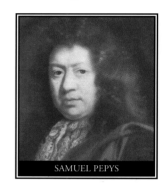

SAMUEL PEPYS

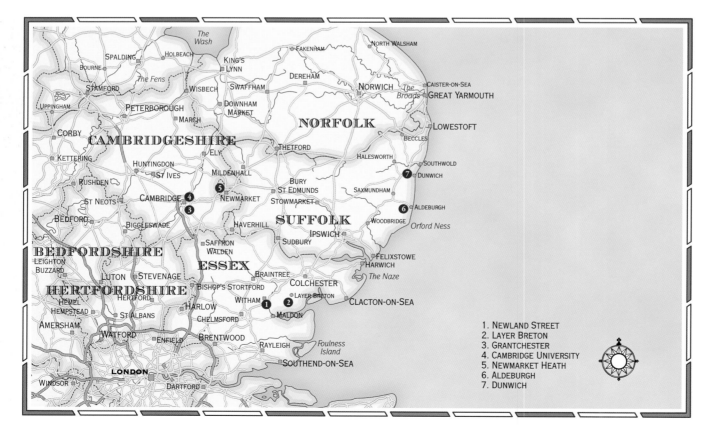

1. NEWLAND STREET
2. LAYER BRETON
3. GRANTCHESTER
4. CAMBRIDGE UNIVERSITY
5. NEWMARKET HEATH
6. ALDEBURGH
7. DUNWICH

Newland Street

WITHAM, ESSEX

Although Dorothy L. Sayers (1893–1957) made her name as a very successful author of detective novels featuring her urbane sleuth, Lord Peter Wimsey, in later life she considered that the medieval and religious subjects that gripped her were much more worthy of her time and effort. These included her play *The Man Born to be King* (1943) and her translations of Dante's *Inferno* (1940) and *Purgatorio* (1953).

Dorothy was born in Oxford (see pages 78–9) and attended Somerville College there, where she studied medieval literature. She wrote novels in order to earn money, starting with *Whose Body?* in 1923, and became

PREVIOUS PAGE: M.R. James was Provost at King's College, Cambridge until 1918. He was a noted scholar of medieval illuminated manuscripts and apocryphal Biblical literature.
BELOW: Dorothy L. Sayers lived in this house in Witham, Essex for almost 30 years. Although renowned as one of the great crime writers of her age, she later preferred to write on more academic subjects.

one of the greatest exponents of the classic 20th-century detective novel. After a spell in London in an advertising agency, which gave her all the background she needed when she came to write *Murder Must Advertise* in 1933, she moved to Witham in Essex in 1929, where she lived at 24 Newland Street until her death in 1957. There is now a statue dedicated to the crime-writer in Newland Street, which stands outside the library containing the Dorothy L. Sayers Centre.

Although Lord Peter's cases took him all over the country, two of the novels that featured the aristocratic detective were set in East Anglia. *The Nine Tailors* (1934) contains highly evocative descriptions of the Fens and some of the old churches found there, while *Busman's Honeymoon* (1937) is set in an old East Anglian house where Lord Peter and Harriet Vane, a character that had many parallels with Dorothy herself (they were both in love with Lord Peter), spend their honeymoon and manage to solve a murder at the same time.

Layer Breton

ESSEX

In the sort of coincidence that crops up so often in detective fiction, one of Dorothy L. Sayers's colleagues lived nearby in Essex. Margery Allingham (1904–66) spent most of her childhood at the Old Vicarage in Layer Breton. Her parents were both professional writers and she recalled that the house usually contained a guest who was 'closeted upstairs working to a press-date'. As a child, she was encouraged to notice her surroundings and communicate her thoughts, and this training paid off because her first novel, *Black-Kerchief Dick* (1923), was published when she was just 17 years old. It was a story of smuggling on the Essex marshes, but Margery soon switched to writing detective novels instead. Her hero, Albert Campion (his name is a horticultural pun on the Scarlet Pimpernel) started off as a bit of a fool, but he became more serious as the books continued. In 1940, Margery was commissioned by her American publishers, Doubleday, to write a very different book. This was *The Oaken Heart* (1941), about the impact of the Second World War on the village of Auburn (which was based on Margery's own village of Tolleshunt D'Arcy). In it, she described a community shaken by the conflict, dealing with evacuees and threatened with a German invasion, but still carrying on regardless.

Grantchester

CAMBRIDGESHIRE

While on holiday in Germany before the First World War, Rupert Brooke was gripped by such a strong yearning for Grantchester, where he had lodgings, that he was compelled to write a poem about the village. At the time, it was called 'The Sentimental Exile', although it is now much better known as 'The Old Vicarage, Grantchester'. In it, Brooke conjures up the idyllic world that he knew here, and asks 'Is there honey still for tea?' There always was, courtesy of the bees that were kept by Mr Neeve, his landlady's husband.

Brooke first came to Grantchester in 1909, having cut a literary swathe through King's College, Cambridge (see pages 66–7), where he was an undergraduate. At first, Brooke stayed at The Orchard, moving to The Old Vicarage in 1910. He bathed in Byron's Pool, which was named after the poet who once visited it, and entertained his friends on the lawn. Brooke was on the fringes of the Bloomsbury Group, and his guests included E.M. Forster, Lytton Strachey and Virginia Woolf. He and Virginia had first met in Cornwall when they were children (see page 12). She stayed with him at The Old Vicarage and they bathed naked in the moonlight in the Granta, an act that caused less of a stir among their friends than Virginia had hoped.

Brooke was already writing and publishing his poetry. *Poems 1911* had a good reception and he contributed to the first two volumes of *Georgian Poetry*, a publication that was a creative rebellion against the Victorian poets. He left Grantchester in 1912, and in 1914 embarked on extensive travels to America and Tahiti while recovering from a nervous breakdown. The First World War intervened and Brooke joined the RNVR in 1914. The conflict gave Brooke new material for his poetry, including 'The Soldier', and he quickly became Britain's favourite war poet. This status was enhanced by tragedy when he died from blood poisoning in 1915. *1914 and Other Poems* was published posthumously that same year.

ABOVE: Rupert Brooke's connections with Grantchester have been immortalized in this pub sign.

BELOW: The quiet peace of Grantchester was much more appealing to Rupert Brooke than the bustle of Cambridge.

In recent years The Old Vicarage at Grantchester has been occupied by former politician and ex-convict Jeffrey Archer (born 1940). Archer has written many best-selling novels, including *Not a Penny More, Not a Penny Less* and three volumes of prison diaries.

Cambridge University

CAMBRIDGE

Each Christmas Eve, friends would gather in the rooms of M.R. 'Monty' James (1862–1936), the Provost at King's College, Cambridge from 1905, and listen while he read them his ghost stories. The fire crackled, the candles spluttered and the listeners' flesh would creep, for M.R. James was one of the greatest exponents of the classic ghost story. Although he is now most famous for such tales, they

There'll never again be a home for me like Cambridge.

E. M. FORSTER, *THE LONGEST JOURNEY*

ABOVE: Charles Kingsley, who wrote *The Water Babies* in 1863, was an undergraduate at Magdalene College from 1838 to 1840 and became Professor of Modern History in 1860.

form only a tiny portion of his literary output – he was also a noted scholar of medieval illuminated manuscripts and apocryphal Biblical literature.

King's College also played a central role in the life of E.M. Forster. He first came here in 1897 to read Classics and History. During his first year he had what he disparagingly called a 'puddling' life, but this improved from his second year as he was given rooms in college and was therefore much more involved in the life of the place. In his fourth year he was elected a member of the Apostles. This was a tremendous accolade because the Apostles formed the intellectual cream of Cambridge, and past members had included Alfred, Lord Tennyson. In Forster's novel *The Longest Journey* (1907), the opening scene describes a meeting of the Apostles. Forster left Cambridge in June 1901 with a moderately good degree and soon embarked on a year-long journey around Europe, which provided inspiration for what was then his half-formed idea to become a writer.

Forster returned to Cambridge in 1927 on a three-year fellowship, but it was not a wild success. However, he was back again in 1946 as an Honorary Fellow and was allowed to live at King's College. This was excellent timing because the lease was up on his beloved home, West Hackhurst (see page 29), and he needed to find somewhere new to live. Forster quickly picked up the threads of life at the university and even joined the Apostles again. He remained a Fellow until just before his death from a stroke in June 1970.

Samuel Pepys spent most of his life amassing his library of over 3,000 books, and before he died he made provision for them to be left to his old Cambridge college, Magdalene. He studied here in 1651–53, having previously been at Trinity Hall, and returned to the college for nostalgic visits in October 1667 and May 1668. He recorded both events in his diary, and noted with pleasure that the beer served in the college buttery was 'the best I ever drank'.

The Pepys' Library is in the Second Court at Magdalene, while the Old Library in the First Court contains manuscripts belonging to three of the college's Honorary Fellows: Thomas Hardy, Rudyard Kipling and T.S. Eliot.

C.S. Lewis (1898–1963) was a Fellow of Magdalen College, Oxford, from 1925 to 1954 and was Professor of Medieval and Renaissance English at Magdalene College, Cambridge, from 1954 to 1963. He wrote several books while working here, including *The Magician's Nephew*, one of his 'Narnia' tales for children, and *Surprised by Joy*, which were both published in 1955. He died here in 1963.

Of course, Magdalene and King's are not the only colleges in Cambridge with literary associations, as generations of writers, poets and critics have come here, whether as students, visiting lecturers or college professors. Among the poets and playwrights who studied here are John Milton (Christ's); Siegfried Sassoon (Clare); Samuel Taylor Coleridge (Jesus); William Wordsworth (St John's); Christopher Marlowe, John Fletcher and John Cowper Powys (Corpus Christi); Rupert Brooke (King's and Trinity); Edmund Spenser (Pembroke); Thomas Gray (Pembroke and Peterhouse); Robert Herrick (St John's and Trinity Hall); and Andrew Marvell, John Dryden, Alfred Tennyson and Lord Byron (Trinity).

Cambridge writers and critics include Hugh Walpole (Emmanuel); Rosamond Lehmann (Girton); Laurence Sterne (Jesus); Horace Walpole, E.F. Benson and Shane Leslie (King's); Charles Kingsley (Magdalene); A.S. Byatt and Margaret Drabble (Newnham); Stephen Fry (Queen's); Malcolm Lowry (St Catharine's); James Frazer, Lytton Strachey and Leonard Woolf (Trinity); and Raphael Holinshed, Leslie Stephen and Ronald Firbank (Trinity Hall).

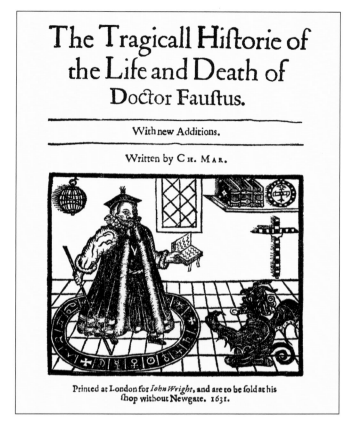

ABOVE: Christopher Marlowe, author of *The Tragedy of Dr Faustus* (1604), studied at Corpus Christi.
BELOW: Samuel Pepys left his massive library to his old college, Magdalene, when he died in 1703.

ABOVE: Scenes like these, of a string of horses in training on Newmarket racecourse, crop up frequently in the crime novels of Dick Francis. He drew on his experiences as a champion jockey.

Newmarket Heath

SUFFOLK

For some reason, East Anglia has long attracted writers of detective and crime fiction: Dorothy L. Sayers, Margery Allingham, P.D. James (born 1920) and Ruth Rendell (born 1930) have all had strong associations with the area. Dick Francis (born 1920) is another noted author who has associations with the region. Francis has written over 30 thrillers, most of which revolve around the sport of horse racing and some of which are set in the Suffolk town of Newmarket.

Dick Francis is such an expert on horse racing because he used to be a champion National Hunt jockey and rode horses owned by the late Queen Mother from 1953 to 1957. After a couple of serious falls he gave up racing and started to write about the sport for the newspapers, before branching out into fiction. His first novel, *Dead Cert*, was published in 1962 and was followed by a book a year. Other jockeys have followed in his literary footsteps, including Bob Champion and John Francome.

Aldeburgh

SUFFOLK

A chain of literary events led the composer, Benjamin Britten (1913–76), to set up the Aldeburgh Music Festival in 1946. He had read an article by E.M. Forster about the 18th-century poet, George Crabbe (1754–1832), who had a strong love of the sea and of the coastal town of Aldeburgh, where he was born. Britten could understand Crabbe's affection for the Suffolk coastline as he had grown up in Lowestoft, a few miles to the north of Aldeburgh, and therefore knew the area well. After reading Crabbe's poem *The Borough* (1810), Britten was inspired to write the opera *Peter Grimes* (1945). It was based on a character from Crabbe's poem, a fisherman overcome with remorse at the way he had treated his apprentices. In 1947, a bust of the poet was erected in the local church.

In 1951, E.M. Forster once again played an important part in Britten's life when he and Eric Crozier wrote the libretto for another Britten opera, *Billy Budd*, which was based on a story by Herman Melville (1819–91), the author of *Moby-Dick* (1851).

Britten, Crabbe and Forster are not the only famous names associated with Aldeburgh. Wilkie Collins

visited the town in 1862 and gave his novel *No Name* (1862) a local setting. He had already written his mystery novel, *The Woman in White* (1860), and followed it with *The Moonstone* in 1868, which is widely claimed to be the first detective novel.

Aldeburgh also appealed to M.R. James, whose ghost stories can still send shivers up the spine of anyone brave enough to read them while sitting alone in a room. As a child, James visited his grandfather here, and towards the end of his life he liked to holiday in Aldeburgh each year.

James claimed that his life-long interest in ghosts began as a child, when he saw a cardboard ghost at a Punch and Judy show. The spectral figure haunted his dreams for years afterwards.

Dunwich

SUFFOLK

In 1855, Edward Fitzgerald (1809–83) brought his great friend, Thomas Carlyle, to the village of Dunwich, on the Suffolk coast overlooking the North Sea. Fitzgerald returned in 1859 while he was busy translating *The Rubáiyát of Omar Khayyám* from the Persian. The first translation was published

ABOVE: Several of P.D. James's crime novels have been set in and around the Suffolk coastline near Dunwich, including *Unnatural Causes* (1967) which opens with a corpse in a boat.

anonymously, but Fitzgerald put his name to the three later revised editions of the poem. Although he wrote other books, he is best remembered for this work.

Fitzgerald and Carlyle were not the only literary figures to come here, as Henry James, Algernon Swinburne (who was inspired to write 'By the North Sea' after his trip to the village) and Jerome K. Jerome (1859–1927), the author of *Three Men in a Boat* (1889), all visited this beautiful stretch of Suffolk's coast.

In 1911, the Canadian author of *Anne of Green Gables* (1908), Lucy Maud Montgomery (1874–1942), visited Dunwich during her honeymoon.

The crime writer P.D. James is another writer who has been inspired by Dunwich, its crumbling cliffs and the surrounding area. The wide, often desolate, beaches of Suffolk are the backdrop to many of her novels and some of them are set around Dunwich, where the aunt of her detective, Adam Dalgliesh, has a house. Naturally, murders take place here, too, and it is certainly an atmospheric setting that seems ideal for James's elegant crime novels.

CHAPTER 5

Central England

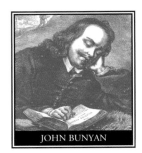

JOHN BUNYAN

Here is a region full of contrasts, from the golden stones of pretty Cotswold villages to the black slag heaps that were produced by Nottingham's coal-mining industry. Laurie Lee charmed millions of readers when he wrote of his idyllic childhood in the tiny village of Slad, while D.H. Lawrence conjured up a harsh picture of grime and death, which was always waiting just round the corner, when writing of his native Nottinghamshire. John Bunyan was imprisoned for his religious beliefs in Bedford gaol, which inspired him to write The Pilgrim's Progress. *Lord Byron had a very different moral code, which he indulged while living in his ancestral home of Newstead Abbey. Some of England's greatest educational establishments are in this part of England, including Eton College, Rugby School and Oxford's dreaming spires, which have inspired writers from Thomas Hardy to Colin Dexter.*

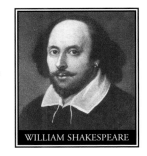

WILLIAM SHAKESPEARE

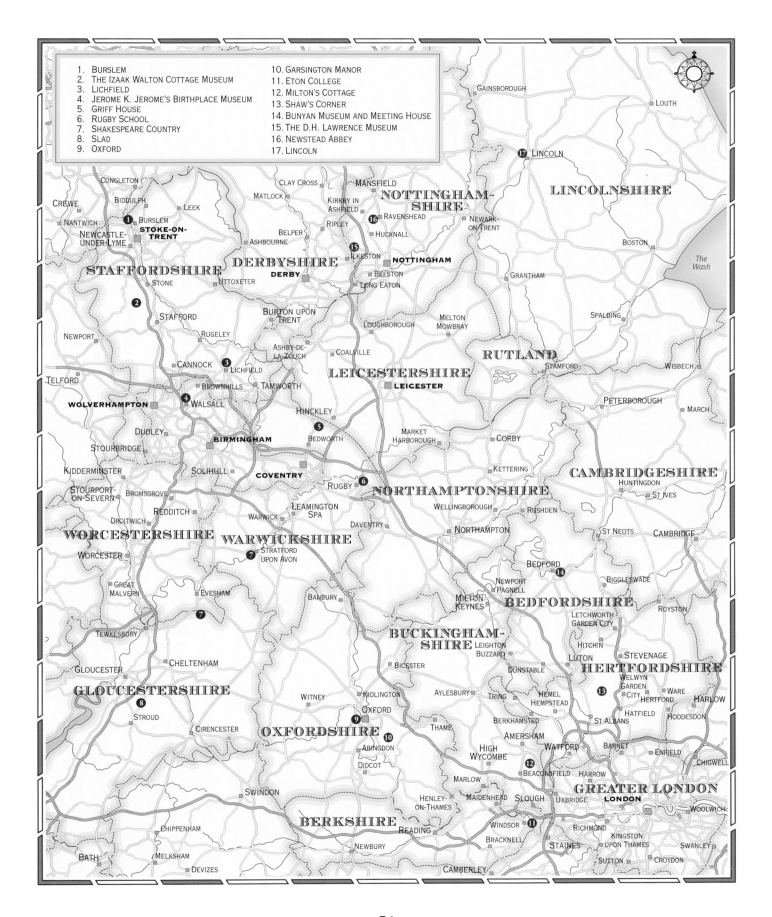

1. BURSLEM
2. THE IZAAK WALTON COTTAGE MUSEUM
3. LICHFIELD
4. JEROME K. JEROME'S BIRTHPLACE MUSEUM
5. GRIFF HOUSE
6. RUGBY SCHOOL
7. SHAKESPEARE COUNTRY
8. SLAD
9. OXFORD
10. GARSINGTON MANOR
11. ETON COLLEGE
12. MILTON'S COTTAGE
13. SHAW'S CORNER
14. BUNYAN MUSEUM AND MEETING HOUSE
15. THE D.H. LAWRENCE MUSEUM
16. NEWSTEAD ABBEY
17. LINCOLN

Burslem

STAFFORDSHIRE

This is one of the 'Five Towns' that feature in Arnold Bennett's novels set in and around the Staffordshire Potteries. However, Bennett renamed them all, so Burslem became Bursley; Hanley (where he was born in 1867) became Hanbridge; Tunstall was transformed into Turnhill; Longton turned into Longshaw; and Stoke-on-Trent became Knype. Bennett's Five Towns, together with Fenton, were united in the borough of Stoke-on-Trent in 1910.

Bennett wrote 13 novels and three collections of short stories about the places where he grew up and the effect that the pottery industry had on the people who lived there. However, his novels were written from memory as he left Staffordshire for London when he was 21, and moved to Paris for ten years in 1902. His first novel, *A Man from the North*, was published in 1898, but Bennett really started to make a name for himself with *Anna of the Five Towns* (1902), which tells the story of a miser's daughter. *The Old Wives' Tale* (1908) was particularly successful and drew on many of his childhood memories. By now Bennett was starting to earn serious money, and he eventually became one of the highest paid writers of his day.

Many of the places in the Five Towns appear in Bennett's novels and stories, and in Burslem some of them are marked by plaques. Burslem Park is mentioned in *Anna of the Five Towns* and in *Clayhanger* (1910). After Bennett died from typhoid in 1931, his ashes were buried in the cemetery at Burslem; the world-famous writer had come home at last.

The Izaak Walton Cottage Museum

SHALLOWFORD, STAFFORDSHIRE

It is a neat irony that many of the details of Izaak Walton's (1593–1683) life have become muddled over the years, because in his day he was a noted biographer. He was born in Stafford, probably in the summer of 1593, and was baptized in St Mary's Church in September of that year – an event that was commemorated by a bust of him in the 19th century.

Walton could barely wait to leave Stafford and move to London, and by the time he was 21 he was running his own business as a linen draper in Fleet Street. He also began writing. His first biography took as its subject the poet John Donne and was published to great acclaim in 1640. It contained the intriguing fact that before Donne died in 1631 a portrait was drawn of him wearing his shroud and standing on a funeral urn, which showed how he thought he would look when he rose from his grave on the Day of Judgement.

All went well for Walton until the start of the English Civil War. He was a Royalist and an Anglican, which was a tricky combination for any well-known author who lived in London, so Walton returned to his native Staffordshire. He particularly enjoyed fishing in the River Dove with his friend, the poet Charles Cotton (1630–87), who lived in Beresford Dale. He also enjoyed writing, and the first edition of *The Compleat Angler, or the Contemplative Man's Recreation* was published in 1653. This was a guide to freshwater fishing, presented as a dialogue between Piscator (a fisherman), Venator (a hunter) and Auceps (a fowler). A year later, Walton bought part of Halfhead Farm in Shallowford, which came complete with a delightful cottage garden. He never lived here on a permanent basis but visited it often.

The Compleat Angler was such a success that an enlarged edition was published in 1655, followed by further revised editions. The fifth and final edition was published in 1676, with a section on fly fishing by Walton's old friend, Charles Cotton.

PAGE 70: In 1665, John Milton and his family took refuge from the Great Plague in a modest cottage in Chalfont St Giles. It is Milton's only surviving residence.

ABOVE: Arnold Bennett immortalized his home town of Hanley as Hanbridge in his series of novels about the Potteries. He left for London in 1889 and became editor of *Woman* magazine in 1896.

ABOVE: Izaak Walton's cottage is now a museum devoted to his memory. It is typical of the 16th and 17th centuries, and is decorated in a style that Walton would have recognized.

On Walton's death in Winchester in 1683 (see page 26), he bequeathed Halfhead Farm to the town of Stafford with the stipulation that the annual rent of £21 should be used for charitable works, including buying coal for the poorest people in the district each winter. His most celebrated book, which had been so popular during Walton's life, was 'rediscovered' by Dr Johnson in 1750, and experienced a further revival of interest in the 19th century.

Walton's cottage was opened as a museum in 1924 and managed to survive two fires in the thatched roof. It is furnished in the style of the late 17th century, when Walton lived here, and contains an angling museum.

Lichfield

STAFFORDSHIRE

Lichfield's greatest literary claim to fame is that it is the birthplace of Dr Samuel Johnson. He was born in 1709 over his father's bookshop in Breadmarket Street, which was a very fitting location for one who grew up to become a writer, critic and the compiler of the first English dictionary. His birthplace is now a museum devoted to his memory and contains copies of his books and many of his belongings. A statue of him, which was erected in 1838, stands in Market Street and there is a statue nearby of Johnson's great friend and biographer, James Boswell (1740–95).

Johnson was baptized in St Mary's Church and took his first lessons at the age of five at Dame Oliver's School in Dam Street. Later, he attended the local grammar school, which originally stood in St John's Street before being moved to Borrowcrop Hill in 1903. In 1728, Johnson went to Pembroke College, Oxford (see pages 78–9), but he could not afford to stay and left just over a year later without his degree. Life was very tough for the next few years, and in 1735 he embarked upon three new ventures: he translated a book from French; he married Mrs Elizabeth Porter, who was much older than him; and he and his wife opened a private school in Edial, near Lichfield. This third enterprise was not exactly the money-spinner he had been hoping for, and in 1737 he left for the greener pastures of London with one of his pupils, David Garrick (1717–79), who became a celebrated actor and remained a good friend of the Johnsons throughout their lives.

Johnson kept up his links with Lichfield. He visited his stepdaughter, Lucy Porter, who lived in the now-demolished Redcourt House in Tamworth Street. When he came to Lichfield with Boswell, the pair stayed at the Three Crowns Inn, which was situated two doors away from Johnson's birthplace.

There are memorials to both Johnson and Garrick in Lichfield Cathedral, which is notable for its three spires, known as 'the Ladies of the Vale'. There is also a memorial to Anna Seward (1747–1809), the poet who was known as 'the Swan of Lichfield' and lived at the Bishop's Palace (her father was the canon of the cathedral) from 1754 to 1809. When Boswell was writing his Life of Samuel Johnson (1791), Seward was able to help him with some of the details.

Nathaniel Hawthorne (1804–64) was another

ABOVE: Lichfield has not forgotten its most famous son, Dr Samuel Johnson. This handsome memorial to him stands in the cathedral, although he was buried in Westminster Abbey.

literary pilgrim who was eager to trace Johnson's life in Lichfield, and he wrote of his visit in *Our Old Home* (1863). He stayed at the Swan Inn, which is where Johnson himself stayed on a journey to Wales.

Jerome K. Jerome's Birthplace Museum

WALSALL, WEST MIDLANDS

Although Jerome K. Jerome's comic novel, *Three Men in a Boat* (1889), made him rich and famous, it also eclipsed everything else he ever wrote. Much of his other work has now been virtually forgotten, even *Three Men on the Bummel* (1900), which was his follow-up to his greatest success.

When *Three Men in a Boat* was first published it was so immensely popular that the humorous magazine, *Punch*, identified it as a rival for the public's affections and immediately lambasted it for its lowbrow wit. Yet such sour grapes could not spoil the success of Jerome's chronicles of the three young clerks who embark on a rowing holiday on the Thames, accompanied by the dog Montmorency.

Jerome Klapka Jerome was born in Belsize House in Walsall in 1859, but his family moved to London when he was four. Nevertheless, he was made a freeman of Walsall in 1927 and his birthplace has since been turned into a museum in his memory.

Griff House

CHILVERS COTON, WARWICKSHIRE

Throughout her life, the novelist George Eliot looked back on her childhood at Griff House (now a hotel) with great affection. She was born Mary Anne Evans in 1819 and her family moved to Griff House when she was five months old. The house included a farmyard and a pool, and it is easy to detect more than a flavour of her childhood home in the opening chapters of *The Mill on the Floss* (1860). Her father managed the estate and he used to take his infant daughter with him when he visited the farm's tenants, which gave her an early education in rural life.

There were many pools, water pumps and canals around Griff House, and this proximity to water certainly influenced Eliot's career as a novelist – water is a recurrent theme in *The Mill on the Floss*. She lived here until the spring of 1841 when she and her father moved to Foleshill in Coventry. Her brother, Isaac, and his new wife, Sarah, moved into Griff House, where they stayed for the rest of their lives. Mary Ann (as she now called herself, although she was to have several more name changes) was the youngest child and it was considered her duty to take care of her widowed father. The fact that she did not want to made her chafe against the conventions of Victorian Britain; a theme that flowed through her later writings and which made her notorious in her later life when she lived openly with her married lover, G.H. Lewes.

The area around Griff House was the inspiration for many places in her novels. She based Shepperton Church in *Scenes of Clerical Life* (1858) on the church at Chilvers Coton, where she was baptized; and Arbury Hall, which was 'the big house' on the estate that her father managed when she was a child, became Cheverel Manor in the same book.

Throughout her eventful life, George Eliot kept fond memories of Griff House, writing in 1874 'I seem to feel the air through the window of the attic above the drawing-room, from which when a little girl, I often looked towards the distant view of the Coton College.' In fact, she spent the rest of her life trying to find a house that would match the perfection of her precious childhood home.

Rugby School

RUGBY, WARWICKSHIRE

Tom Brown's Schooldays was published in 1857. The title page announced that it was by 'An Old Boy'. The old boy in question was Thomas Hughes, who attended the school from 1834 to 1841. His novel makes no bones about his admiration for the

then headmaster, Dr Thomas Arnold (1795–1842), who pioneered what became the public school system in Britain. Hughes championed what became known as 'muscular Christianity', which combined a strong Christian belief with prowess on the sports field, loyalty to one's school and country, and courage. All these matters were encouraged at Rugby, and Dr Arnold had many devoted old boys who followed these ideals all their lives. His pupils included his son Matthew (1822–88), who later became the poet and champion of secondary education; A.P. Stanley (1815–81) who nailed his pro-Arnold colours to the mast when he wrote *The Life and Correspondence of Thomas Arnold* (1844), and the poet Arthur Clough (1819–61). Later pupils at Rugby included Walter Savage Landor; Charles Dodgson (Lewis Carroll); Rupert Brooke, who was born in Hillmorton Road and whose father was a housemaster at the school; Arthur Ransome

ABOVE: Mary Ann Evans, who wrote as George Eliot, was never a conventional 19th-century woman. There are many similarities between her and Maggie Tulliver of *The Mill on the Floss* (1860).

BELOW: When Thomas Hughes attended Rugby School in the 1830s it had recently been rebuilt and Dr Thomas Arnold was headmaster. His schooldays made a profound impression on him.

ABOVE: Shakespeare's Birthplace on Henley Street has been refurbished as accurately as possible to recreate the interiors as they might have been in the 1570s.

(1884–1967), the author of *Swallows and Amazons*; Wyndham Lewis (1882–1957); and Salman Rushdie (born 1947).

Shakespeare Country

STRATFORD-UPON-AVON, WARWICKSHIRE

Shakespeare and Stratford. The words go together like Romeo and Juliet or any of the hundreds of other phrases that entered the English language after Shakespeare wrote them. This is the old market town where William Shakespeare (1564–1616) was born, educated and married, and where he later lived having made enough money to buy the biggest house he could find.

William Shakespeare was born in a half-timbered house in Henley Street. The exact date of his birth, as with so much of his life, is disputed, but it is generally believed to be 23 April. This is rather neat as it is also St George's Day, which commemorates the patron saint of England, and it is also the date on which Shakespeare died in 1616.

The bedroom in which Shakespeare is thought to have been born is not only interesting in its own right, but has the added attraction of some literary graffiti on the window where such luminaries as Sir Walter Scott, Isaac Watts and Thomas Carlyle scratched their names.

Only the foundations and the garden remain from New Place, which was Shakespeare's last home. However, Hall's Croft, the home of his daughter Susanna and her husband, Dr John Hall, is well worth visiting. Mary Arden's House, which was the home of Shakespeare's mother, is at Wilmcote, just outside Stratford, and Anne Hathaway's Cottage at Shottery was the family home of Shakespeare's wife.

When Shakespeare died in 1616 he was buried in the chancel of Holy Trinity Church, under an epitaph that he is said to have written:

Good friend for Jesus sake forbeare
To digg the dust enclosed heare
Blest be ye man yt spares hes stones
And curst be he yt moves my bones

It is tempting to imagine that Stratford is nothing but one huge monument to Shakespeare, but there are other literary links even if most of them do lead back to the great man sooner or later. Washington Irving

(1783–1859), the satirist and poet, stayed at the Red Horse in Bridge Street in 1818, under the assumed name of Geoffrey Crayon, and wrote about his visit in *The Sketch-Book of Geoffrey Crayon, Gent.* (1819–20). Marie Corelli (1855–1924), who specialized in romantic melodramas, moved to Stratford in 1901 in the hope that proximity to the Bard's memory would stimulate her creativity. She is believed to be the inspiration for E.F. Benson's larger-than-life character Lucia, who originally lived at Riseholme near Stratford before moving to Tilling (see page 36). Although Marie Corelli became a figure of fun long before she died in 1924, she was instrumental in preserving Harvard House, which was built by the grandfather of John Harvard, the founder of Harvard University. Samuel Clemens (1835–1910), who wrote as Mark Twain, was delighted by the house when Marie showed it to him in 1907.

Mrs Gaskell first ventured into print when she wrote about Stratford in William Howitt's *Visits to Remarkable Places* (1840). She knew the town, having attended Avonbank School there, which has long since vanished.

Slad

GLOUCESTERSHIRE

ABOVE: The little village of Slad, clinging to the side of a hill, was Laurie Lee's home when he was a small boy, and his autobiographies captured all its charms and problems.

Laurie Lee's lyrical account of growing up in Slad, *Cider with Rosie* (1959), describes a lost world. It tells of the English countryside between the two World Wars, abundant with flowers and sweet grass, where large families were crammed into a few rooms, and choirboys trekked through the snow each Christmas to earn money from carol-singing. There were the two grannies who lived next door to each other in a permanent state of war and, of course, Rosie who introduced the young Laurie to the delights of cider.

Laurie Lee (1914–97) arrived in Slad in 1917 when he was three, and 'there with a sense of bewilderment and terror my life in the village began'. He was frightened by the grass, which he had only ever seen at a distance until that moment and which towered over his head. He left for London when he was 19, and then went to Spain on a journey that he describes in *As I Walked Out One Midsummer Morning* (1969),

which was the second book in his autobiographical trilogy. After the success of *Cider with Rosie*, Lee was able to return to Slad in the 1960s with his wife, Cathy, and he stayed here until his death. He lived near his local pub, the Woolpack Inn. The final part of the trilogy, *A Monument of War*, was published in 1991.

It is quite obvious from Lee's prose that it is written by a poet, and he published several volumes of verse, including *The Sun My Monument* (1944) and *The Bloom of Candles* (1947).

... blades of heat and bursts of cuckoos, and the garden is a turmoil of bees and scratching hens

LAURIE LEE, *I CAN'T STAY LONG*

ABOVE: It was only on rare occasions that Charles Lutwidge Dodgson would admit to being Lewis Carroll. He was always offended if anyone alluded to his other identity.

Oxford

OXFORDSHIRE

From Dorothy L. Sayers to Colin Dexter (born 1930), Percy Bysshe Shelley to Philip Larkin (1922–85), Lewis Carroll to Philip Pullman (born 1946), Oxford fairly bristles with literary connections. Many writers attended university here and then wrote about it, while others never studied here but wrote about the city anyway.

Thomas Hardy turned Oxford into Christminster in *Jude the Obscure* (1896), and the eponymous character lodged in the Jericho area of the city. Evelyn Waugh (1903–66) was an undergraduate at Hertford College and transformed his experiences into a nostalgic, golden idyll in *Brideshead Revisited* (1945). The novel combined snobbery and Roman Catholicism, which were two of Waugh's guiding principles.

Dorothy L. Sayers drew on her time as an undergraduate at Somerville for her detective novel, *Gaudy Night* (1935), in which Harriet Vane solves a mystery at her old college while being wooed by Lord Peter Wimsey, a character who also knew Oxford well, having been created a Balliol man. More recently, fans of Colin Dexter, who lives in the city, have developed a useful knowledge of Oxford through his detective novels, which feature the irascible Inspector Morse and his trusty sergeant, Lewis.

Charles Dodgson became Master and tutor at Christ Church in 1855, and taught here for the rest of his life. The world knows him better as Lewis Carroll, who immortalized his young friend, Alice Liddell, in *Alice's Adventures in Wonderland* (1865) and *Through the Looking Glass and What Alice Found There* (1871). Other writers who went to Christ Church include the Elizabethan poet Sir Philip Sidney (1554–86), John Ruskin and W.H. Auden (1907–73), who was later Professor of Poetry here and lived in a cottage in the grounds in the early 1970s.

William Morris was at Exeter College from 1853 to 1855, and 40 years later his writings enthralled a young Exeter undergraduate called J.R.R. Tolkien (1892–1973), who was particularly inspired by Morris's translations of Icelandic sagas. He spent over 30 years as a Professor at Exeter, and also found time to create his own world of Middle Earth in *The Hobbit* (1937) and *The Lord of the Rings* (1954–55). Tolkien was a colleague of C.S. Lewis, who was a Fellow at Magdalen College from 1924 to 1954. While he was at Oxford, Lewis wrote many books including *The Screwtape Letters* (1942) and began the Narnia stories that made him world-famous.

Sir John Betjeman, accompanied by his beloved teddy bear, Archibald, was a contemporary of Lewis at Magdalene College. He described his time at Oxford in his verse-autobiography *Summoned by Bells* (1960). While he was here he became friends with a group of poets that included Auden and Louis MacNeice (1907–63), who went to Merton College. He also mixed with Stephen Spender (1909–95), who was at University College, and Cecil Day-Lewis, who was at Wadham College. Day-Lewis and Auden edited *Oxford Poetry* in 1927, and in the 1950s Day-Lewis became Professor of Poetry here. He wrote about his

Oxford life in *The Buried Day* (1960).

To young readers, Oxford is synonymous with Philip Pullman's trilogy of children's books *The Northern Lights*, *The Subtle Knife* and *The Amber Spyglass*, which are set partly in the city we know but also in an alternative and fantastical Oxford. Having said that, to some extent every novel that has ever been written about Oxford could be described as a fantasy in its own way.

Garsington Manor

GARSINGTON, OXFORDSHIRE

Between 1915 and 1928, Garsington Manor was the home of Philip and Lady Ottoline Morrell, who were members of the Bloomsbury Group (see page 54). Lady Ottoline was one of the great society hostesses of her day and she delighted in filling her Elizabethan manor house with the cream of the youthful literary set, and especially in adopting them as her protégés. It was considered quite an honour to be invited here, and guests included such luminaries as Lytton Strachey;, Siegfried Sassoon; D.H. Lawrence; John Maynard Keynes; T.S. Eliot; Clive Bell; Katherine Mansfield; John Middleton Murry; Bertrand Russell (with whom Lady Ottoline had a long-running affair); and Aldous Huxley.

However, in 1921 Huxley was considered to have bitten the hand that fed him following the publication of his first novel, *Crome Yellow*. Crome, the house he described in the novel, was obviously based on Garsington, and the main characters, Henry and 'Old Priscilla' Wimbush were undoubtedly Philip and Ottoline. They were not the only ones to have been used as literary fodder, because Huxley drew heavily on the characteristics of many of his literary contemporaries,

including Lytton Strachey and his devoted friend, Dora Carrington.

Lady Ottoline, with her long, horse-like face and strange clothes, was an irresistible target for writers of the period and for those who came later. D.H. Lawrence turned her into Hermione Roddice in *Women in Love* and she was the inspiration for Lady Sybilline Quarrell mentioned in *Forty Years On* (1968), a play by Alan Bennett (born 1934).

BELOW: Garsington Manor, home of the society hostess Lady Ottoline Morrell, was turned into Crome by Aldous Huxley in his novel *Crome Yellow* (1921); Lady Ottoline was not pleased.

ABOVE: Eton College is the proud owner of numerous first editions by its literary alumni, who include Ian Fleming, Aldous Huxley and George Orwell.

BELOW: This edition of *Paradise Lost* (1667) is one of the books on display at Milton's Cottage. He first conceived the desire to write an epic poem in 1639 but did not begin it until 1658.

Eton College

WINDSOR, BERKSHIRE

This is probably the most famous school in Britain, if not the world. It has the distinction of having been founded by Henry VI (1422–71) in 1440, and later enjoyed the patronage of George III (1760–1820). The list of distinguished Old Etonians is endless and even includes the fictional character of James Bond. This is hardly surprising as his creator, Ian Fleming, was an Old Etonian, as was his brother, Peter.

Percy Bysshe Shelley (1792–1822) came to Eton in 1804 and kept himself busy by being rebellious, conducting scientific experiments and writing the gothic novel *Zastrozzi* (1810). Other Old Etonian poets include Thomas Gray; Algernon Swinburne; Robert Bridges; Sir Osbert and Sir Sacheverell Sitwell; and Hugo Williams. Many other writers are Old Etonians, including Henry Fielding; Horace Walpole; Anthony Powell; George Orwell; Cyril Connolly, who wrote about his schooldays and much else in *Enemies of Promise* (1938); Robin Maugham; Nicholas Mosley; Aldous Huxley, who also taught here from 1917 to 1919; M.R. James (who became Provost in 1918); John Lehmann; James Lees-Milne; Nigel Nicolson; and Henry Green (whose real name was Henry Yorke).

Milton's Cottage

CHALFONT ST GILES, BUCKINGHAMSHIRE

Although this is called 'Milton's Cottage', the great poet only spent a short time here from 1665 to 1666. Its importance comes from being the only home of the poet's to have survived.

John Milton (1608–74) brought his family to Chalfont St Giles in 1665 to escape the plague, which was just starting to ravage London. It was a wise move, as this turned out to be the Great Plague that killed thousands of Londoners rather than the usual bout of the disease, which afflicted London each summer. The move to the countryside was orchestrated by Thomas Ellwood (1639–1713), who was a pupil of Milton's.

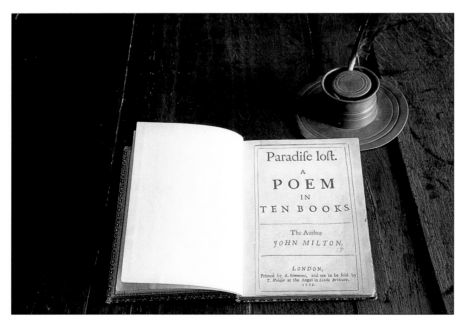

Paradife loft.
A
POEM
IN
TEN BOOKS.

The Author
JOHN MILTON.

LONDON,
Printed by S. Simmons, and are to be fold by
T. Helder at the Angel in Little Britain.
1669.

Ellwood described the cottage as 'that pretty box in St Giles, Chalfont'.

Despite Milton's rather difficult marriage to Elizabeth Minshull (it was his third) and his blindness, he managed to put the finishing touches to *Paradise Lost* (1667) while at the cottage. It was a return to poetry after having spent some time writing political pamphlets and meant that he no longer had to fear a knock at the door from the authorities. Milton had strong Republican sympathies, which were perfectly acceptable during the Civil War and Commonwealth of the 1640s and 1650s, but such beliefs saw him imprisoned after the Restoration in 1660 when he published his pamphlet *The Ready and Easy Way to Establish a Free Commonwealth*.

The cottage garden at Milton's Cottage is planted with many of the flowers that Milton mentions in his poetry. Completely blind, as he had been since 1651, probably as a result of glaucoma, Milton could not see the flowers that grew here, but he would have been able to smell them and have them described to him. It seems fitting that he composed his epic poem about the fall of Adam and Eve from the Garden of Eden while surrounded by the scents and sounds of an English garden.

ABOVE: For years, George Bernard Shaw and his wife, Charlotte, were not very taken with their home in Ayot St Lawrence, yet they spent decades here. Their ashes were scattered in the garden.

BELOW: Shaw was a prodigious writer and worked in the summerhouse in the garden at Shaw's Corner. Charlotte rationed the number of callers so he could work in peace.

Shaw's Corner

AYOT ST LAWRENCE, HERTFORDSHIRE

It took over two years for the playwright George Bernard Shaw and his wife, Charlotte, to find what would become Shaw's Corner. They lived in London after their marriage in 1898 and the move to the countryside was something of a compromise between a wife who loathed work and enjoyed carting her husband off on foreign trips for the sake of his health, and a husband who loathed travel and wanted to be allowed to get on with his work.

When the Shaws first found the house, which they remained in for the rest of their lives, it was the local rectory and neither of them much liked it. However, the rector could not afford to stay here so they rented it, reminding each other that they would

ABOVE & BELOW: The stained-glass windows in the Bunyan Meeting House in Bedford depict scenes from *The Pilgrim's Progress*. John Bunyan wrote part of the book while in prison.

not be living here for long. In 1904 they moved in, and were still here 14 years later when they finally bought the house.

Initially, the villagers of Ayot St Lawrence took little interest in Shaw's celebrity as a writer – his first successful play *John Bull's Other Island* was performed in 1904 and became a big hit. They were also unsure of him as a man, as they wondered if he were entirely respectable. Such suspicions increased after he attracted notoriety and threats of violence during the First World War with the publication of his anti-war pamphlet *Common Sense about the War* (1914). Shaw was finally accepted by the village in 1915 when he helped to clear up after the great Hertfordshire Blizzard, which laid waste to the surrounding countryside. Villagers began to refer to the house as Shaw's Corner, and the name stuck.

A great puzzle about Shaw was the startling difference between his private self and the publicity-hungry 'G.B.S.', who trumpeted his ideas on social reform with as much noise as possible. In fact, his G.B.S. persona, which he considered to be an invention, was a mask he was able to hide behind. Shaw took great delight in delivering a talk to the local Women's Institute called 'How to Quarrel Properly'. He saw the importance of taking daily exercise, but was reluctant to venture beyond the gates of his house, so he and Charlotte walked around the garden, marking the number of laps they had completed with pebbles placed on a windowsill until they had walked the required distance of one mile.

Shaw wrote in the garden, in a spartan hut-cum-summerhouse, which he called 'the wilderness'. It had a revolving base so he could follow the sun, and was heated by an electric stove in the winter. He became a generous benefactor of the village, although no one was allowed to breathe a word about it.

Charlotte died in September 1943, and people who did not understand Shaw fully were astonished by his grief; at times he cried openly in public, apparently unable to stem the flow of tears. In September 1950, he went out into the garden after sunset to prune a greengage tree, but slipped and broke his thigh. He was operated on at the local hospital, to which he sent a very generous cheque for the staff. He went home to Shaw's Corner where he died at the beginning of November. He had already arranged to leave the house to the National Trust and it was opened to the public the following spring with Shaw's belongings still in it. He once wrote 'we die because we do not know how to live', but his engaging, quirky spirit lives on at Shaw's Corner.

ABOVE: D.H. Lawrence was born at 8A Victoria Street, now a museum, in 1885, but his family did not stay here long because his mother was keen to move to a better neighbourhood.

Bunyan Museum and Meeting House

BEDFORD, BEDFORDSHIRE

John Bunyan (1628–88), who is most famous as the author of *The Pilgrim's Progress* (1684), was a minister in Bedford from late 1671 until his death. He first became a preacher in 1653, but fell foul of the powers-that-be in November 1660 for preaching without a licence and spent most of the next 12 years in Bedford Gaol. The site of his former imprisonment is marked at the point where Silver Street and the High Street meet. Nearby, at the corner of St Peter's Street and the Broadway, is Sir Joseph Boehm's bronze statue of Bunyan with his Bible in his left hand.

Bunyan did not allow imprisonment to slow him down, and he wrote nine books during his stay in Bedford Gaol, including *Grace Abounding to the Chief of Sinners* (1666), which tells the story of his life and how he found God. Bunyan was released from prison in 1672, but was briefly incarcerated again in 1676, during which period he once again put pen to paper. This time, the result was the first part of *The Pilgrim's Progress*, which was published in 1674; he completed it

in 1684. Many of the places mentioned in the book are modelled on those in and around Bedford, such as Stevington Cross where Christian dropped his burden.

The original barn where Bunyan preached has long since vanished and been replaced by the Bunyan Museum, which contains some of Bunyan's belongings as well as copies of his books.

The D.H. Lawrence Museum

8A VICTORIA STREET, EASTWOOD, NOTTINGHAMSHIRE

David Herbert Lawrence was born here on 11 September 1885. He was the fourth child of an illiterate father and an educated mother. This mismatch between his parents caused immense friction within the family because his mother, an ex-schoolteacher, wanted her son to escape the almost inevitable working-class fate of having to follow his father down the mines. The Lawrence family was poor but they managed to better themselves in stages, each time moving to a slightly more genteel area of Eastwood.

Once he had moved away from Nottingham, Lawrence described it as 'the country of my heart', but this was a classic case of distance lending enchantment to the view because he disliked it when he lived here. For one thing, the smoky air did nothing for his weak lungs and he twice became ill with pneumonia. For another, he did not fit in with his contemporaries, thanks to his interest in literature and his mother's desire to shake the coal dust off her family's shoes.

Lawrence won a scholarship to Nottingham High School, which he attended from 1898 to 1901, and then left at the age of 16 to work as a clerk in a Nottingham factory. This phase ended after he developed pneumonia and it was while he was convalescing that he met Jessie Chambers, who encouraged him to write. His first short story was published in the local paper in 1907, while he was training to be a teacher at University College, Nottingham.

After another bout of pneumonia in 1911, Lawrence decided to abandon teaching for full-time writing. This year was a turning point for him emotionally, too, because he met and fell in love with Frieda Weekley, the German wife of his old professor at Nottingham. She left her husband and children in the spring of 1912 and ran away with Lawrence, first to Germany and then to Italy. Lawrence married Frieda in London in July 1914, 'with neuralgia in my left eye and my heart in my boots'. It was to be a tempestuous marriage.

No. 8A Victoria Street, where Lawrence was born, is now a museum in his memory, and is decorated and furnished in a style he would have known. There are also exhibitions about him and his travels.

Newstead Abbey

NOTTINGHAMSHIRE

George Gordon, Lord Byron (1788–1824) was the great literary celebrity of his day. He was a baron, having inherited the title in 1798 at the tender age of ten. He owned Newstead Abbey, a 12th-century estate that had been in the family since 1540 and which was in a romantically dilapidated state of repair. He was wildly handsome, which always helps in most matters and in this case distracted people from his club foot. And he was a celebrated poet, having taken the literary world by storm with the first two cantos of *Childe Harold's Pilgrimage* in March 1812. As he later commented, 'I awoke and found myself famous'. Byron was also notorious for his revolutionary politics – for example, he believed that Greece should be freed from Turkish rule – and his outrageous affairs with many women. The most shocking of these was his very close relationship with his half-sister, Augusta Leigh. If this was not actual incest it looked very much like it, and neither protagonist did anything to dispel people's suspicions. Byron also knew how to throw a party, and the revels he hosted at Newstead Abbey raised the eyebrows of the local worthies, especially when they heard that one of the drinking vessels was a skull-goblet.

By the time Byron was 24, in 1812, he had travelled widely and scored a notable success with *Childe Harold*. That same year he met his future wife, Annabella Milbanke; started what became a red-hot affair with Annabella's cousin, Lady Caroline Lamb; and had affairs with two other women. He also managed to find enough time to write more verse, including *The Giaour* and *The Bride of Abydos*, which were both published in 1813. This was another notable year for Byron because it was supposedly when

BELOW: When Lady Caroline Lamb first met Lord Byron she described him as 'Mad, bad and dangerous to know.'

he began an affair with Augusta. Their relationship scandalized society, and when Augusta gave birth to a daughter in 1814, society reached the shocking conclusion that Byron was her father. Elizabeth Medora, the offspring in question, later added fuel to this particular fire by stating that Byron was definitely her father.

Byron married Annabella in January 1815 and their daughter, Ada, was born that December. However, the marriage was over by January 1816. The scandal surrounding this parting, coupled with Byron's acute financial difficulties, forced him to leave England in April 1816. He put Newstead Abbey on the market but it took two years to sell, and was finally bought for £94,500 by Thomas Wildman, an old school friend of Byron's.

After leaving England, Byron went first to Geneva where he became friendly with Percy and Mary Shelley, and then went on to Venice. Naturally, he managed to have affairs in each city. He also wrote two more cantos of *Childe Harold*, and began *Don Juan* (1819).

In 1820, Byron became involved in the Italian revolution against the Austrians, and in late 1823 the whiff of revolutionary politics enticed him to Greece. However, he contracted malaria and died in Missolonghi in April 1824. His body was returned to England and buried in the Byron family vault at Hucknall Torkard Church, near Newstead Abbey. His half-sister, Augusta, erected the memorial to him in the chancel. He left his memoirs, which he wanted to be published after his death, but a group of his friends burned them – they doubtless felt that his life had been quite scandalous enough without him leaving documentary evidence of the shocking things that had really happened.

Newstead Abbey is open to the public and one of the most popular sights is the grave of Byron's favourite

ABOVE: After his death, a statue was erected to Alfred, Lord Tennyson outside Lincoln Cathedral. Many of his most famous poems are concerned with loss, mourning and death.

dog, Boatswain, who died in 1808. In a typical act of irreverence Byron had the monument built where he believed the High Altar of the original priory church to have once stood.

Lincoln

LINCOLNSHIRE

Just as Lincoln Cathedral dominates the area for miles around, so the statue of Alfred, Lord Tennyson by George Frederick Watts (1817–1904) dominates the city's Cathedral Close. It is entirely fitting that Tennyson should be commemorated in this way, as he was a son of the county and always retained strong links with it. Many documents, books, photographs and other artefacts connected with Tennyson are housed in the Tennyson Room in Lincoln's Usher Gallery and in the Tennyson Research Centre in Lincoln Central Library.

Tennyson was born in Somersby in Lincolnshire in August 1809, the fourth of 12 children born to the Reverend George Clayton Tennyson and his wife, Elizabeth. He grew up in his father's rectory at Somersby and started to write poetry from an early age: he had completed an epic poem of 6,000 lines by the time he was 12 years old.

The young Tennyson was strongly influenced by the poetry of George Gordon, Lord Byron, and was devastated by the news of his death in 1824. In 1833, Tennyson was once again consumed with grief when his dearest friend, Arthur Hallam, died. He began to write *In Memoriam*, a long elegy for his friend, which was not published until 1850, the year after he became Poet Laureate.

The statue of Tennyson was erected in the Cathedral Close at Lincoln after his death in 1892, in memory of his Lincolnshire upbringing.

CHAPTER 6
Northern England

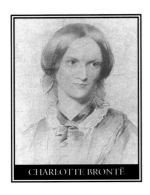

CHARLOTTE BRONTË

Stretching from Yorkshire up to Cumbria and Northumberland, this area has some of the most spectacular scenery in England. It is hardly surprising, therefore, that for centuries it has attracted writers and poets who are inspired by the landscape, from Bram Stoker whose gothic imagination was fired by an incident during a visit to Whitby in North Yorkshire, to the Romantic poets who flocked to the Lake District in a movement that was headed by William Wordsworth and Samuel Taylor Coleridge. A country vet's practice in Thirsk proved the inspiration for a series of best-selling novels by James Herriot, while the dramatic countryside around Haworth and a difficult home life prompted a creative outpouring from Charlotte, Anne and Emily Brontë.

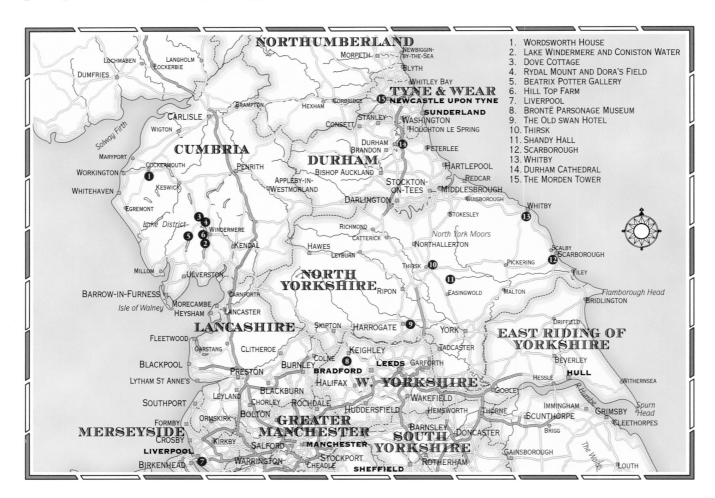

1. WORDSWORTH HOUSE
2. LAKE WINDERMERE AND CONISTON WATER
3. DOVE COTTAGE
4. RYDAL MOUNT AND DORA'S FIELD
5. BEATRIX POTTER GALLERY
6. HILL TOP FARM
7. LIVERPOOL
8. BRONTË PARSONAGE MUSEUM
9. THE OLD SWAN HOTEL
10. THIRSK
11. SHANDY HALL
12. SCARBOROUGH
13. WHITBY
14. DURHAM CATHEDRAL
15. THE MORDEN TOWER

Wordsworth House

COCKERMOUTH, CUMBRIA

In his poem *The Prelude* (1850), William Wordsworth described many of the memories of his childhood, including the delight he took in the River Derwent as it ran past the foot of the house in which he grew up. We now know this residence as Wordsworth House, although it was never owned by the Wordsworth family. They were tenants of Sir James Lowther, the local landowner who employed John Wordsworth, William's father, as his land agent.

William Wordsworth was born here on 7 April 1770, and his devoted sister, Dorothy, arrived here on Christmas Day 1771. They were close all their life and in his poem, 'The Sparrow's Nest', Wordsworth described her as 'The Blessing of my later years'.

Wordsworth developed his love of literature from spending hours in his father's library at Wordsworth House. His father encouraged him to learn vast tracts of Shakespeare, Spenser and Milton by heart. It was

a happy childhood until 1778 when Wordsworth's mother, Ann, died. Dorothy was packed off to stay with some relatives in Halifax and did not see her favourite brother, William, again for nine years. Wordsworth and his two brothers were educated at the grammar school in nearby Hawkshead (see page 92).

Wordsworth House ceased to be the family home when John Wordsworth died suddenly at the end of 1782. It was the end of Wordsworth's life at Cockermouth, but it was not the end of his life in the Lake District.

Lake Windermere and Coniston Water

CUMBRIA

Cumbria's Lake District has inspired poets and novelists for centuries, whether they visited the area on precious holidays or actually lived here.

PREVIOUS PAGE: St Mary's churchyard at Whitby was one of the settings in Bram Stoker's *Dracula* (1897) – Count Dracula, in the guise of a dog, visits the churchyard in search of prey.

BELOW: William Wordsworth spent the first eight years of his life in what is now called Wordsworth House, although at the time his family only rented the property.

Arthur Ransome, the children's author, was born in Leeds, but his father carried him up Coniston Old Man when he was only a few weeks old and it was the start of his lifelong love affair with the area. As a small boy he attended a preparatory school called Old College in Windermere; he went on to attend Rugby (see pages 75–6) and enjoyed family holidays around High Nibthwaite. From these cosy beginnings Ransome went on to become an intrepid traveller and journalist who covered the Russian Revolution first-hand and whose second wife, Evgenia Shelepina, was Trotsky's secretary.

Ransome was already a published author when he began *Swallows and Amazons* (1930), which was his first novel for children. It covered what was then the unusual topic of children's holidays and was a slow seller, as was *Swallowdale* (1931). Ransom's persistence finally paid off with the publication of *Peter Duck* in 1932, and he suddenly found that he was the author of a best-selling series. He wrote 12 children's novels chronicling the adventures of the Swallow (Walker) and Amazon (Blackett) families, who spent much of their time in the Lake District. Although Ransome never specified the location of 'that great lake in the North', it is an amalgam of Lake Windermere and Coniston Water. Equally, Wild Cat Island appears to be a mixture of Blakeholme in Lake Windermere and Peel Island in Coniston Water.

One of Ransome's friends was W.G. Collingwood, secretary to John Ruskin, who was one of the greatest

ABOVE: In 1825, a regatta was held on Lake Windermere to celebrate Sir Walter Scott's 54th birthday. It was organized by the author John Wilson (1785–1854), who had a house nearby.

Victorian critics, poets and artists. Both Ruskin and Collingwood lived on Coniston Water, although Ruskin's house, Brantwood, was by far the finer of the two and it also had magnificent views of the lake.

Ruskin lived at Brantwood, which is now open to the public, from 1871 until his death in 1900. He is buried in St Andrew's churchyard, Coniston, under a tall cross of Tilberthwaite stone, which was designed by Collingwood. Collingwood set up the Ruskin Museum in Coniston, in honour of his friend.

Dove Cottage

GRASMERE, CUMBRIA

When William Wordsworth (1770–1850) and his devoted sister, Dorothy (1771–1855), moved into Dove Cottage on 20 December 1799, they hoped to enjoy a quiet, idyllic existence here. They had spent many years apart but, now both in their late twenties, they wanted to live together in rural bliss. Dove Cottage was small and simple, with stone walls and a roof of local slate. It had been a pub called the Dove and Olive until 1793, when it was converted

ABOVE: William and Dorothy Wordsworth moved into Dove Cottage just before Christmas 1799 and immersed themselves in the natural beauty of their surroundings.

between 1800 and 1803, is a vivid description of life at Dove Cottage and also served as inspiration for her brother's poetry. His poem, 'Home at Grasmere', recalls the delight he took in his sister's company while they were living at Dove Cottage.

Life, of course, rarely works out as planned, and in October 1802 this fraternal companionship was shattered when William brought his bride, Mary Hutchinson, to live at Dove Cottage. Children soon followed, and their three eldest, John, Dora and Thomas, were all born in the downstairs bedroom at Dove Cottage.

Wordsworth was not the only poet to live in the Lake District at the time. His great friend, Samuel Taylor Coleridge (1772–1834), moved to Keswick with his family in 1800 and was a frequent visitor to Dove Cottage. Since 1797, when they first met, Coleridge, Wordsworth and Dorothy had enjoyed an intensely creative partnership that contributed greatly to the rise of the English Romantic Movement, but the relationship became strained in the Lake District. Coleridge fell in love with Sara Hutchinson, who came for long visits to help her sister look after the children, and he eventually left his wife for her in 1807. He was also in the grip of his addiction to opium, which finally led to a rift with the Wordsworths that never entirely healed.

By 1808, Dove Cottage had become far too small for the Wordsworths and their extended family, which now included another poet, Thomas De Quincey. Wordsworth had composed some of his greatest poems in the cottage, including 'Intimations of Immortality from Recollections of Early Childhood', but it was time to leave. They moved to Allan Bank, a house at the foot of Easedale, where

into a modest house. It was all the Wordsworths could afford, despite the legacy of £900 that William had been left by his friend, Raisley Calvert.

Dorothy tended the garden, where she grew vegetables and flowers, and William helped her when he was not writing. Dorothy's *Journal*, which she kept

The thought of her was like a flash of light
Or an unseen companionship, a breath
Or fragrance independent of the wind

WILLIAM WORDSWORTH, 'HOME AT GRASMERE'

Coleridge and De Quincey stayed with them during their first winter there. In the spring of 1809, the Wordsworths leased Dove Cottage for De Quincey, who remained its tenant until 1834 even though he no longer lived here. Like Coleridge, De Quincey was addicted to opium, and celebrated his addiction in his 1822 book *Confessions of an English Opium Eater*.

Rydal Mount and Dora's Field

AMBLESIDE, CUMBRIA

William Wordsworth and his sister, Dorothy, often walked to the post box in Ambleside from their home at Dove Cottage (see pages 89–91) in Grasmere. In 1813 the Wordsworth household, which by this time had grown to include William's wife, Mary, and their three surviving children, moved to Rydal Mount in Ambleside. Two of their children had died in 1812, during their tenancy of the Old Rectory opposite St Oswald's church in Grasmere, and the Wordsworths could no longer bear the sight of their graves in the churchyard.

Wordsworth lived at Rydal Mount for the rest of his life. It is where he composed almost half his poems and, in doing so, established his reputation as one of the greatest poets of the 19th century. As his fame grew, so did the number of distinguished visitors who flocked to Rydal Mount to meet him, including Matthew Arnold and Nathaniel Hawthorne. The poet Algernon Swinburne also came to Rydal Mount, although he was only 11 at the time, and was moved when Wordsworth told him 'I do not think, Algernon, that you will forget me.'

Wordsworth was made Poet Laureate in 1843, following the death of Robert Southey (1774–1843), who had lived nearby at Greta Hall in Keswick. Southey grew to hate his job as the nation's poet, which he held for 30 years, but Wordsworth had a much shorter stint because he died in 1850 after catching a chill while taking a walk. The post then went to Alfred, Lord Tennyson. Wordsworth was buried in St Oswald's churchyard, where his two children had been laid to rest so many years before. His wife, Mary, died in 1859 and shares his grave. The

BELOW: Rydal Mount was Wordsworth's home for the last 37 years of his life. Although his literary powers waned as he grew older, he was made Poet Laureate in 1843.

churchyard also contains the graves of their children, Dora and William, and that of Dorothy Wordsworth who died in 1855.

Rydal Mount is open to the public and contains many of Wordsworth's possessions, plus many first editions of his books. The main bedroom gives a good view of neighbouring Dora's Field, which is a stretch of land that Wordsworth bought when he feared his tenancy of Rydal Mount would not be renewed; he planned to build a house on the plot. In the event, there was no need because the tenancy continued without interruption, and he gave the land to his daughter, Dora. It is now planted with thousands of daffodils, which erupt each spring in a flowery riot that evokes the first line of one of Wordsworth's most famous poems, 'I wandered lonely as a cloud'.

Beatrix Potter Gallery

HAWKSHEAD, CUMBRIA

In the early 1900s, this was the office of William Heelis, who was the local solicitor. One of his clients, who relied on his legal skills whenever she bought property in the surrounding area, was Beatrix Potter (1866–1943), and they married in October 1913. Potter could afford to buy up farms and land because she was making so much money from her career as a noted children's author (see below).

The building has been kept much as it was when Heelis worked here, and there is a reconstruction of his office. However, the main purpose of the building is to exhibit some of the many original drawings and illustrations that were created by his wife. She not only authored and illustrated the books she wrote for children, which made her world-famous, but also wrote many private letters.

Hawkshead has another literary connection: William Wordsworth attended the Free Grammar School here from 1779 to 1787, after which he went to St John's College, Cambridge. It was originally thought that he lodged with Mrs Anne Tyson in Hawkshead while he was at the school, but some clever detective work by Beatrix Potter revealed that the Tyson family had moved from Hawkshead to nearby Colthouse in about 1773, and, therefore, that Wordsworth had lived with them there instead.

Hill Top

NEAR SAWREY, CUMBRIA

Beatrix Potter first visited the Lake District in 1882 when she was 16, and it was the start of a lifelong love affair with this part of England. It was sheer chance that brought her here. She and her parents usually spent their summers in Scotland, but when the house they normally rented became unavailable they opted for Cumbria instead. They returned in following years, during which Beatrix gained a vivid impression of the area by watching and sketching the wildlife and the countryside. The charm of the Lake District inspired Beatrix to write stories about it, and her first book, *The Tale of Peter Rabbit*, was published in 1902. Two more books, *The Tailor of Gloucester* and *Squirrel Nutkin*, swiftly followed in 1903. All of the books were both written and illustrated by her.

Beatrix now had an income of her own, and in 1903 she bought a

THIS is what those little rabbits saw round that corner!
Little Benjamin took one look, and then, in half a minute less than no time, he hid himself and Peter and the onions underneath a large basket...

40   41

OPPOSITE: Hill Top delighted Beatrix Potter when she moved here in 1905. At last she was able to escape the claustrophobic demands of her parents, although never for long.
LEFT: Beatrix Potter's *The Tale of Benjamin Bunny* was inspired by her first pet rabbit, Benjamin Bouncer who had a passion for hot buttered toast.

field in Near Sawrey, where she and her family had taken their holiday that year. In 1905, she used the royalties from *Peter Rabbit* to buy the small farm of Hill Top. Beatrix lived and worked here for the next eight years, and Hill Top was the home of both Tom Kitten in *The Tale of Tom Kitten* (1907) and Samuel Whiskers in *The Tale of Samuel Whiskers* (1908), while the local pub, The Tower Bank Arms, appeared in *The Tale of Jemima Puddle-Duck* (1908).

Hill Top was Beatrix's artistic inspiration, which was priceless to her in itself, but it also provided her with a means of gradually separating herself from her family's tight grasp. In October 1913, when she was 47, she married her solicitor, William Heelis (see page 92), much to the opposition of her parents who made it plain that they believed her rightful duty was to look after them. In 1909, Beatrix had bought Castle Farm in Sawrey, and this became the couple's marital home, while she continued to work at and from her adored Hill Top.

However, Beatrix's love of farming left her with little time for writing and painting, and she only wrote four more books in her lifetime. The phenomenal and continuing success of her children's stories enabled her to buy a total of 4,000 acres of land, plus 15 farms in which she encouraged the breeding of Herdwick sheep. This rare breed is indigenous to the Lake District, and in 1943 Beatrix achieved the remarkable feat of becoming the first woman to be elected President of the Herdwick Sheepbreeders' Association; however, she died before she could take up her position.

On her death, Beatrix Potter left all her land to the National Trust. It was a charity dear to her heart and, curiously enough, one of the founders was Canon Hardwicke Rawnsley, who was the local vicar when Beatrix first visited the Lake District and who encouraged her to publish her stories. Hill Top was also part of her bequest to the National Trust, with the proviso that it should be left exactly as it was when she was alive, and perhaps it is this comfortable, homely atmosphere that makes it one of the most popular tourist attractions in the Lake District.

ABOVE: The role of Liverpool and its docks, such as the Albert Dock above, in the Second World War inspired Nicholas Monsarrat (1910–79), who was born in Rodney Street in the city, to write *The Cruel Sea* (1951).

Liverpool

MERSEYSIDE

When Daniel Defoe visited Liverpool while collecting copy for his three-volume guidebook *A Tour through the Whole Island of Great Britain* (1724–26), he was very impressed with 'the Fineness of the Streets and the Beauty of the Buildings'. Thomas De Quincey, who made short visits to the city in 1801 and 1803, was struck by its international flavour and referred to it as 'the many-languaged town'.

Even then, Liverpool was an important sea port that received many imported goods, but its customs men were perplexed in 1819 when William Cobbett (1763–1835) revealed that his luggage contained the bones of his great hero, Thomas Paine. Paine, the revolutionary English writer who helped to draft the American Declaration of Independence, had been buried unceremoniously in unconsecrated ground near New York in 1809. His supporters had hoped to raise enough money for a proper monument to him, but they failed to do so and Cobbett felt he had no option but to transport Paine's remains back to England himself. Unfortunately, history is silent on what eventually happened to Paine's bones – perhaps they are lying forgotten in a piece of 19th-century luggage.

Other transatlantic travellers whose ships docked at Liverpool included Mrs Harriet Beecher Stowe (1811–96), who stayed with Matthew Arnold's brother-in-law, Mr Cropper, at Dingle Bank in 1853. Her anti-slavery novel, *Uncle Tom's Cabin*, had been published the year before to great sensation, and this was the first of three visits she made to Britain. Herman Melville (1819–91), who had spent some time in Liverpool in 1837 when he was a cabin boy on a sailing ship, returned in 1856 for a few days before sailing to Constantinople. By this time he had written several books, including *Moby-Dick* (1851), which virtually sank without trace when it was published and continued to be overlooked until the 1920s.

Charles Dickens knew Liverpool well, not only as a visitor, but also as a performer at St George Hall Concert Room, the Philharmonic Hall and the Theatre Royal, among other venues. In 1842 he sailed from Liverpool for America, and recorded some of his thoughts about the country in *Martin Chuzzlewit* (1844). America was not amused by what he had to say.

Liverpool has had many home-grown writers, too. Beryl Bainbridge was born here in 1934. She was expelled from school for writing rude limericks, but has since written many books that draw on her Liverpudlian childhood as well as many other experiences.

Willy Russell, who made his name as the author of such hit plays and musicals as *Educating Rita* and *Blood Brothers*, was born in Liverpool in 1947. Many of his productions have been performed at the Liverpool Everyman theatre. Alan Bleasdale (born 1946), his almost exact contemporary, has written novels and short stories as well as many plays, screenplays and television series, including *Boys from the Blackstuff* (1980).

Liverpool achieved global fame in the early 1960s with the rise of the Beatles and other Merseyside pop groups. At the same time, it was cultivating a trio of poets who became almost as famous: Brian Patten (born 1946), Roger McGough (born 1937) and Adrian Henri (1932–2000), collectively known as the Liverpool Poets, whose anthologies included *The Mersey Sound* (1967). The three of them were awarded the Freedom of the City of Liverpool in 2002, although Henri received the honour posthumously. Poets continue to thrive in Liverpool, including Paul Farley whose *The Ice Age* (2002) won the Whitbread Poetry Prize in 2003.

Brontë Parsonage Museum

HAWORTH, WEST YORKSHIRE

This is surely one of the most romantic literary settings in Britain. It conjures up images of a troubled family to whom death was no stranger, but which proved a fertile breeding ground for the talents of Charlotte (1816–55), Anne (1820–49), Emily (1818–48) and Branwell (1817–48) Brontë. There are reminders of these many family tragedies in the graveyard and church, where all the Brontë family lie with the exception of Anne who died and was buried in Scarborough (see pages 97–8).

The Brontë siblings grew up in Haworth Parsonage, where their father was Perpetual Curate. Their mother, Maria, died of cancer in 1821 and was buried in the church. In 1825, she was joined there by her two eldest daughters, Maria and Elizabeth, who both died of consumption. This disease was the scourge of the 19th century, and it flourished in the chilly, damp northern climate.

The three remaining Brontë daughters all worked as governesses, but their real love was writing. They first ventured into print in 1846, with a collection of their poems which was published at their own expense under the pseudonyms of Currer, Ellis and Acton Bell. Although they only sold two copies of their book, it acted as a creative catalyst for them and triggered a fever of writing. *Jane Eyre*, by Charlotte, was published in October 1847 to immediate acclaim, and was followed by Anne's *Agnes Grey* and Emily's *Wuthering Heights* two months later. Anne's second novel, *The Tenant of Wildfell Hall*, was published the following summer. All the novels drew heavily on the sisters' life in Yorkshire, and were considered deeply shocking in some quarters because they dealt with such themes as adultery, obsessive love and alcoholism. The women had experience of the latter through their brother, Branwell.

The literary outpourings of this tight family group did not last long because both Branwell and Emily died from tuberculosis in 1848, followed by Anne in 1849. Charlotte continued to write novels and in 1854 she married her father's curate, Arthur Bell Nicholls, but she died in March 1855 during the early stages of pregnancy. Her friend, the novelist Mrs Gaskell, published her biography, *Life of Charlotte Brontë*, in 1857.

BELOW: After the deaths of her three siblings, Charlotte Brontë was left at Haworth with her father. She had to wait for two years before he gave her permission to marry his curate.

The Old Swan Hotel

HARROGATE, NORTH YORKSHIRE

In December 1926, Britain was gripped by a mystery that could have come straight from the pages of one of Agatha Christie's detective stories. Christie herself, a highly successful crime novelist since the publication of her first novel, *The Mysterious Affair at Styles*, in 1920, had disappeared. At the time she was married to Colonel Archie Christie and they lived in a house called Styles (after the house in her first novel) in Sunningdale, Berkshire. Agatha's Morris Cowley was found abandoned at Newlands Corner, near Guildford in Surrey, but there was no trace of the novelist herself. The story was splashed all over the newspapers, and readers of the *Daily News* were offered a reward of £100 for any information that would lead to the discovery of Agatha, whether dead or alive.

The police were involved and interviewed Colonel Christie on suspicion of murder. However, there was no body, and members of the public were invited to help the police search for Agatha's corpse at Newlands Corner on 12 December. They did not find anything.

At this moment of supreme drama, word reached a reporter of the *Daily News* that the missing Mrs Christie was staying in Yorkshire at the Harrogate Hydro, which has since changed its name to The Old Swan Hotel. He raced up to the Yorkshire town, followed closely by the police and Colonel Christie, who formally identified the woman staying at the hotel under the name of Mrs Teresa Neele as his wife. Sensation! The press swarmed over the hotel, demanding interviews with the novelist, but her husband refused to allow her to speak to the press and excused her behaviour with a single word – 'amnesia'.

This excuse was far from the truth, some of which soon came out in the press. Colonel Christie was having an affair with a Miss Nancy Neele, and had asked Agatha for a divorce on the morning of her disappearance. This explained the surname adopted by

ABOVE: Speculation is still rife about why Agatha Christie disappeared in 1926 only to be found staying at a hotel in Harrogate under an assumed name.

Agatha in Harrogate. But why Teresa? The press decided that this was because it was an anagram of 'teaser'. The Christies divorced in 1928 and Archie married Nancy Neele a few weeks later.

Thirsk

NORTH YORKSHIRE

When Alf Wight (1916–95) started to write his reminiscences of life as a country vet in Yorkshire in the 1940s and 1950s, he had no idea what he was embarking on. He hoped that he might find a publisher and that people would enjoy reading his book, but thought no further than that. His first book, *If Only They Could Talk*, was published in 1970 and was a phenomenal success. It was followed by *All Creatures Great and Small* in 1972 and many more. Always a modest man, Wight chose the pseudonym James Herriot, and continued to practise as a vet in Thirsk. He wrote his books in his spare time and they became increasingly successful, spawning a popular television series and a film. If he had hoped for anonymity he was disappointed because fans managed to discover who he was and where he worked, and used to beat a path to his door.

Although Wight lived and worked in Thirsk, he invented a series of place names for his books, which revolved round the fictional town of Darrowby. It has much in common with Thirsk, but borrows from several other Yorkshire towns, including Richmond. Wight's surgery at 23 Kirkgate has now been turned into The World of James Herriot, complete with veterinary equipment from the 1940s and 1950s.

Shandy Hall

COXWOLD, NORTH YORKSHIRE

When Laurence Sterne (1713–68) called his new home Shandy Hall, he was being ironic as it was anything but grand, being a medieval priest's house that had been extended in the

17th century. Such a joke was entirely characteristic of Sterne, who was the reverse of what his name suggested and who also refused to conform to the standard image of how an 18th-century vicar should behave. His books, most of which he wrote in the study at Shandy Hall, also caused quite a rumpus.

Sterne moved here in 1760 when he was made perpetual curate of St Michael's Church, Coxwold. The first two volumes of his first novel, *The Life and Opinions of Tristram Shandy*, had been published the previous year and he was still enjoying their success and notoriety. Sterne stirred up further moral outrage in 1760 with the publication of *The Sermons of Mr Yorick* (a character from the previous novel) followed by further volumes of *Tristram Shandy* in 1761, 1765 and 1767. The novel itself was an art form that was still in its infancy at this point. However, this rambling work is generally thought to be the novel in which stream-of-consciousness originates, a style of writing that found favour with such 20th-century writers as Virginia Woolf and James Joyce. In 1768, Parson Yorick appeared in print once again as the narrator of *A Sentimental Journey through France and Italy*.

Sterne died of tuberculosis in London that same year. His death spawned a rash of forgeries written in his name, including more volumes of *Tristram Shandy* and *A Sentimental Journey*.

ABOVE: Laurence Sterne, who lived at Shandy Hall during the last years of his life, wrote *Tristram Shandy* 'under greatest heaviness of heart' caused by his wife's mental breakdown and his parents' deaths.

Shandy Hall fell into disrepair, but it was rescued in the 1960s and lovingly restored to its 18th-century appearance. Some of the rooms and gardens are open to the public.

Scarborough

NORTH YORKSHIRE

In the spring of 1849, Anne Brontë visited Scarborough in the company of her sister, Charlotte, and her friend, Ellen Nussey. The seaside town was a particular favourite of Anne's, but she had not travelled here for pleasure; instead, she had come in a last-ditch attempt to stave off the tuberculosis that was doing its best to kill her. On 28 May 1849, she died at 2 The Cliff, a building that has since been demolished to make way for the Grand Hotel. She was buried in St Mary's churchyard.

Another important literary family is linked with Scarborough. The Sitwell siblings, Edith (1887–1964),

Whitby

NORTH YORKSHIRE

Legend has it that Bram Stoker (1847–1912) conceived the idea for his gothic chiller, *Dracula* (1897), when he was sitting on the cliffs above Whitby Bay. He watched a ship sailing into the harbour and immediately his imaginative processes started working – here was the ship that would bring Count Dracula to England from Transylvania and enable him to turn the innocent Lucy into a fellow member of the 'Un-Dead'.

In the novel, Dracula disembarks in the shape of a big black dog and heads for St Mary's churchyard, which is a favourite sitting place of Mina, a young woman on whom Dracula has designs. Stoker's novel was influenced by 'Carmilla', a short story about a female vampire from *In A Glass Darkly* (1872) by Sheridan Le Fanu (1814–73), and in its turn *Dracula* launched a flourishing industry of vampire films and books that continues to this day.

Whitby had already appeared in print when *Dracula* was published. Mrs Gaskell wrote about the town in *Sylvia's Lovers* (1863), although she called it Monkshaven, and changed the name of St Mary's Church to St Nicholas. She got a good feel for the town after spending a couple of weeks at 1 Abbey Terrace in 1859.

The Reverend Charles Lutwidge Dodgson (Lewis Carroll) was another Victorian visitor to the town. He came here several times between 1854 and 1871, and stayed at what is now Barnard's Hotel in East Terrace.

ABOVE: Sir Osbert Sitwell's six volumes of autobiography shed light on his troubled relationship with his father, Sir George.

Osbert (1892–1969) and Sacheverell (1897–1988), knew the town well as children because their mother's family owned a house here, Londesborough Lodge. In 1887, Edith was born next door in Wood End, The Crescent, which was her parents' seaside home; it is now a natural history museum. Edith's younger brother, Sacheverell, was born ten years later in Belvoir Terrace. Osbert's novel, *Before the Bombardment* (1926), described the shelling of Scarborough during the First World War. He later claimed that it was his favourite novel – could this be in part because his parents, with whom he had a love-hate relationship (mostly veering towards the latter), experienced the shelling at first hand while staying at Wood End? Osbert was so attached to the novel that, at his request, a copy of it was buried with him.

Wood End was a favourite place of the novelist, Susan Hill, who was born in Scarborough in 1942 and attended Scarborough Convent School between the ages of three and sixteen. She wrote about the town in her novel, *A Change for the Better* (1969), and later in *Family* (1989). Wood End features in her short story 'In the Conservatory' from *A Bit of Singing and Dancing* (1973).

For lovers of the stage, Scarborough is synonymous with the Stephen Joseph Theatre, where virtually every play by Alan Ayckbourn (born 1939) receives its première as he is the artistic director there.

Durham Cathedral

COUNTY DURHAM

This is the final resting place of both St Cuthbert (died 687) and the Venerable Bede (c. 673–735), and therefore contains the bones of the chronicled and the chronicler respectively. St Cuthbert was the 7th-century Bishop of Lindisfarne who preferred the life of a hermit to that of an evangelist but accepted the task that he had been given. He retired to his hermitage on the island of Inner Farne, where he died in AD 687. He was buried in Lindisfarne and later canonized. His tomb immediately became associated with miracles and therefore attracted many pilgrims.

When the monks fled Lindisfarne during the Viking raids of AD 875 they obeyed St Cuthbert's instructions to take his bones with them, and his remains were eventually taken to Durham where a church was built especially for them. This church later evolved into Durham Cathedral, which was built between 1093 and 1135. St Cuthbert was given a special, richly decorated shrine in the cathedral, but this was damaged and sacked in 1540 during the Reformation and the saint now lies beneath the simple grey stone tomb that is inscribed 'Cuthbertus', which is all that Henry VIII's henchmen left behind.

St Bede spent most of his life in St Paul's monastery at Jarrow. It was his home town, having been born there in about AD 672, and he never strayed too far from it. He wrote many religious books, including commentaries on some of the books and gospels in the Bible, as well as books on ecclesiastical music. And, of course, he wrote *The Life and Miracles of St Cuthbert, Bishop of Lindisfarne*, which many historians believe is a rather generous account of the saint's life, peppered with stories of an astonishing number of miracles.

Of the 40 or more books written by the Venerable Bede, as he became known in the 9th century, the most famous is his *Historia Ecclesiastica Gentis Anglorum*, or *Ecclesiastical History of the English People*, which he completed in AD 731. It describes the history of the English from the invasion of Julius Caesar until the 730s, and it is still a valuable source of information about Anglo-Saxon England.

Durham Cathedral also contains many important medieval archives in the Durham University Library, which can be found in the precincts of the cathedral and can be viewed by arrangement.

The Morden Tower

NEWCASTLE-UPON-TYNE, TYNE AND WEAR

The Morden Tower has nestled in the West Walls of Newcastle-upon-Tyne since it was built in about 1290. Despite having survived for so long

ABOVE: Beautiful Durham Cathedral has many important medieval archives in the Durham University Library; it also has the Chapter Library, the Archdeacon Sharp Library and the Meissen Library.

it was in a terrible state when it was leased as a venue for poetry readings in 1964. After it was repaired, the round upper room in the tower became an important showcase for poets.

In December 1965, Basil Bunting (1900–1985) gave the first reading of his semi-autobiographical poem, *Briggflatts*, which was published the following year. He already had a strong following as a modernist poet in other countries, thanks to the publication of *Redimiculum Matellarum* (1930) in Milan and *Poems* (1950) in Texas, but failed to make much impact on British poets until *Briggflatts* appeared in print.

A string of poets followed Bunting to the Morden Tower, including Ted Hughes (1930–98), Seamus Heaney (born 1939), Allen Ginsberg (1926–97), who in the 1960s declared that Liverpool was 'the centre of consciousness for the entire human universe', and the Liverpool Poets: Brian Patten, Adrian Henri and Roger McGough.

CHAPTER 7

Southern Scotland

R.L. STEVENSON

The southern part of Scotland runs south from the Firth of Forth to the border with England, and is dominated by its two great cities – Glasgow and Edinburgh, which both have strong literary connections. Southern Scotland is also dominated by several literary figures who crop up again and again in this part of the country, especially Sir Walter Scott, whose statue in Princes Street looks out over Edinburgh and whose collection of 'Waverley' novels gave their name to the city's main railway station.

Robert Burns is another literary giant who has many connections with this part of Scotland, as he was born in Alloway and died in Dumfries. Robert Louis Stevenson also has links with this region, as has James Boswell. Southern Scotland is associated with more modern authors, too, such as Hugh MacDiarmid who was a leading member of the so-called Scottish Renaissance of the 20th century.

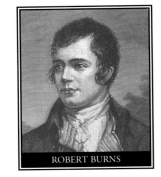

ROBERT BURNS

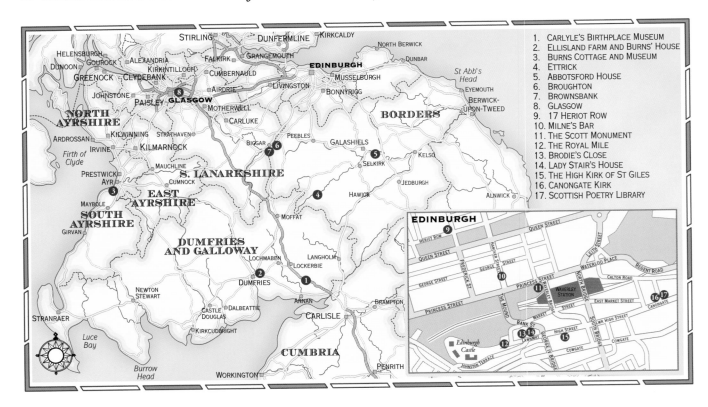

1. CARLYLE'S BIRTHPLACE MUSEUM
2. ELLISLAND FARM AND BURNS' HOUSE
3. BURNS COTTAGE AND MUSEUM
4. ETTRICK
5. ABBOTSFORD HOUSE
6. BROUGHTON
7. BROWNSBANK
8. GLASGOW
9. 17 HERIOT ROW
10. MILNE'S BAR
11. THE SCOTT MONUMENT
12. THE ROYAL MILE
13. BRODIE'S CLOSE
14. LADY STAIR'S HOUSE
15. THE HIGH KIRK OF ST GILES
16. CANONGATE KIRK
17. SCOTTISH POETRY LIBRARY

PREVIOUS PAGE: Lady Stair's House in Edinburgh contains the Writers' Museum, a fascinating collection of memorabilia that celebrates the work of Stevenson, Scott and Burns.

LEFT: Thomas Carlyle, later known as 'the sage of Chelsea', was born in the Arched House in Ecclefechan in 1795. He later taught in the nearby town of Annan before moving away.

Carlyle's Birthplace Museum

ECCLEFECHAN, DUMFRIES AND GALLOWAY

Thomas Carlyle was born in 1795 in the Arched House, which was built by his father and uncle, who were both master masons. His father, James Carlyle, held religious and moral beliefs that were as rigid and unyielding as the stone he worked with, and the young Thomas grew up in a powerfully Calvinist atmosphere, which inevitably had a major influence on him. His parents educated him at home until he was five, after which he attended the village school, progressing to the Annan Academy when he was nine. After going to the University of Edinburgh, Carlyle returned to Annan, where he taught from 1814 to 1816. He continued to teach after leaving Annan, but he also started to write. Carlyle's *Life of Schiller* was published in the *London Magazine* in 1823–24, and appeared in book form in 1825.

At the time, Carlyle was still living in Scotland. In 1826, he married Jane Baillie Welsh, despite her once telling him in a letter that she was his friend but 'your wife! never never!' Money was very tight and the Carlyles began their married life in Edinburgh, before moving to Jane's farm in Craigenputtock, which was a much cheaper proposition altogether.

In 1834, the Carlyles moved to Cheyne Row (see pages 48–9) in London, where they remained for the rest of their lives. This was also the point at which Carlyle's literary career really took off with the publication in 1833–34 of *Sartor Resartus*. When Carlyle died in 1881 he was known as the 'sage of Chelsea', and was so respected that straw was put down in the street so that noise from the passing horses' hooves would not disturb the dying man.

Upon his death there was an immediate demand that he should be buried in Westminster Abbey (see pages 53–4), but he had requested that he should be buried back home in the Ecclefechan churchyard. Carlyle's wishes were carried out – something that did not always happen to dead Victorian writers who hoped to avoid literary deification in the abbey. He was buried beside his parents and a statue was erected in his memory in the village in 1927. The Arched House is now a museum replete with Carlyle's belongings and memorabilia.

Ellisland Farm and Burns' House

DUMFRIES

The great Scottish poet Robert Burns (1759–96) spent the last few years of his life in Dumfries. Just like his father, William, who had built the family home at Alloway (see page 104), Burns built the farmhouse at Ellisland Farm. Today, a Burns museum is open to the public on the site, which is north of Dumfries and is where Burns lived with his family from 1788 to 1791. This was a productive period for him in terms of writing verse, and he composed over 130 poems and songs while living here, but in terms of farming it was a disaster. His health was failing, the soil was poor to the point of exhaustion and Burns finally gave up on the whole enterprise. Farming had not worked out for his father and it did not prosper for Robert, either. He wrote to his brother, Gilbert, 'It is a ruinous affair… let it go to hell.' Instead, Burns began to work as an excise officer, which involved collecting taxes and made him highly unpopular in the district, in addition to which he was unfairly accused of political disloyalty.

Burns moved to Dumfries in 1791 with his wife, Jean Armour, and their children, where they lived in what is now called Burns' House, which is also open to the public. He was never a faithful man – he fathered 12 children by four different women – and while living in Dumfries had an affair with Annie Park, the barmaid at the Globe Inn, who became pregnant. When her child was born it became another member of the Burns household.

Years of backbreaking farming and trying to coax productivity out of uncooperative soil had damaged Burns' health, and at Dumfries he became ill with rheumatic fever. He died at Burns' House in July 1796, a few days before Jean gave birth to their son, Maxwell, who was born on the day of Burns' funeral. And what a funeral it was,

attended by thousands after Burns' body had lain in state in the Midsteeple in the High Street. Burns was buried in a simple grave in St Michael's churchyard, but his coffin was exhumed in 1815 and reburied in a special mausoleum, which was adorned with a statue of the poet, in another part of the churchyard. All the great poets of the day flocked to visit the Scottish bard's grave. William Wordsworth wrote a poem about the first 'grass grown' grave entitled 'At the Grave of Burns', and John Keats later visited the mausoleum, which he found was 'not very much to my taste', although he wrote a sonnet, 'On Visiting the Tomb of Burns', about it.

BELOW: The chair in which Robert Burns wrote his last poems is on display in the spartan study of Burns' House in Dumfries.

ABOVE: Although he is now one of the most famous Scots poets to have ever lived, Robert Burns was born into humble beginnings in what is now called Burns Cottage.

BELOW: St Mary's Loch is near Tibbie Shiel's Inn, where James Hogg, popularly called 'the Ettrick Shepherd', used to meet his mentor, Sir Walter Scott. Scott had a passion for Scottish ballads.

Burns Cottage and Museum

ALLOWAY, SOUTH AYRSHIRE

The many millions of people who celebrate Burns Night each 25 January, traditionally with haggis and whisky, are commemorating an event that took place in a whitewashed, thatched cottage on 25 January 1759, when a baby son was born to William Burns and his wife, Agnes. They called him Robert and he was the first of their seven children. Life was tough for the family, who lived in the two-room building that William had built himself in 1757. Nevertheless, young Robert learned to read and write and attended Alloway School.

In 1766, William became a tenant farmer, first at Mount Oliphant near Alloway and, in 1777, at Lochlie Farm, Tarbolton. His son helped him whenever his schoolwork allowed. However, poor harvests and overwork took their toll, both financially and physically, and William died in 1784. He was buried in Alloway Kirk, which is now in ruins, and is where Robert Burns later set much of his poem 'Tam o' Shanter'.

The Burns family moved to Mossgiel Farm, near Mauchline. It was a formative time for Robert, not only because the death of his father meant he was now head of the family, but because he wrote several poems, including 'To A Mouse', 'Holy Willie's Prayer', 'The Jolly Beggars' and 'The Holy Fair'. His first collection of poems, *Poems, Chiefly in the Scottish Dialect*, was published in 1786 and became extremely popular, but he could not afford to leave farming and later moved to Ellisland Farm, near Dumfries (see page 103), with his wife, Jean Armour, and their two children.

Burns Cottage is open to the public, and there is also a two-room museum devoted to Burns' memory and containing many of his possessions. Many of the places associated with him in Alloway now come under the umbrella of the Burns National Heritage Park, including the Burns Monument.

Ettrick

BORDERS

A tall monument decorated with a bronze medallion marks the birthplace of the Scottish poet James Hogg (1770–1835), who was known as 'the Ettrick Shepherd'. He grew up in Ettrick and was forced to leave school at the age of seven when his father, a sheep farmer, went bankrupt. The young James became a cowherd and later a shepherd. Astonishingly for one who had such an unpromising beginning, Hogg was later able to combine working as a shepherd with a career as a professional writer.

Hogg eventually met Sir Walter Scott who was looking for suitable ballads and poems to include in *Minstrelsy of the Scottish Border* (1802). Scott liked what Hogg sent him and encouraged him to write more. After Hogg's early poems were published in *The Mountain Bard* (1807) he made his name with *The Queen's Wake* (1813). Hogg also wrote novels, including *The Private Memoirs and Confessions of a Justified Sinner* (1824).

Throughout all this he remained close to Scott, and often met him and other writers at Tibbie Shiel's Inn between St Mary's Loch and Loch of the Lowes. Later writers continued to flock here, including Thomas Carlyle and Robert Louis Stevenson. According to legend, Scott and Hogg met for the last time at the Gordon Arms Hotel, near Mountbenger, where the walls of the bar are decorated with framed fragments of some of Scott's letters.

After Scott died in 1832, Hogg wrote *The Domestic Manners and Private Life of Sir Walter Scott* (1834). Hogg himself died the following year, prompting William Wordsworth to write 'Upon the Death of James Hogg' in tribute. Hogg is now remembered in many places around Ettrick, and there is an exhibition about him at Aikwood Tower, which his family once owned, near Ettrickbridge, as well as some information about him in Scott's Courtroom (now a museum) in Selkirk.

Abbotsford House

MELROSE, BORDERS

'It is a kind of conundrum castle to be sure [which] pleases a fantastic person in style and manner.' So wrote Sir Walter Scott (1771–1832) of Abbotsford House, which he spent 13 years converting into the sort of romantic, Scottish baronial fantasy that was the ideal architectural equivalent of his many novels.

Scott was 40 when he first found Cartley Hole Farm in Melrose in 1811. It was a modest farmhouse, and Scott soon demolished it and started to build a bigger house, which he named Abbotsford. This stage of building lasted from 1816 to 1818. Scott also began to purchase adjoining parcels of land, often for more money than they were worth. The increasing amounts of land made the new house seem too small, and the situation was not helped by the many guests who stayed here, including the writers Washington Irving, Maria Edgeworth (1768–1849) and the painter J.M.W. Turner (1775–1851).

When Scott was awarded a baronetcy in 1818 he decided that Abbotsford did not reflect his new status, so once again the builders were called in and they worked on creating a much grander manor house. Scott poured a great deal of money into the project, which was completed in 1824. He had to work harder than ever to finance his building plans, and found other ways of raising the required money as well. He took advances from his publisher for several novels that he had yet to write, and also borrowed from his printer, of which he was a silent partner. In 1826, the inevitable happened when both his publisher and his printer experienced financial crises. Instead of paying off their loans, their money had gone into helping Scott finance the building work at Abbotsford. Scott was left with debts of £120,000, but his creditors could not get their hands on Abbotsford because he had already put it in his son's name.

Work was the answer, and Scott started to write a relentless succession of books. It was the beginning of his decline, both personally and professionally. His wife, Charlotte, died in May 1826 and Scott's already poor state of health became worse. His narrative

BELOW: Sir Walter Scott lived beyond his means at Abbotsford House, which was quite a feat considering he was the most celebrated writer of his day and also one of the most prolific.

powers were also waning, and his last successful novel was *The Fair Maid of Perth* (1828) even though he continued to write until 1831. He had a stroke that same year and, although he recovered enough to be able to visit Italy, his health deteriorated to such an extent that he eventually had to be cared for in the dining room of Abbotsford, where he died in September 1832.

Abbotsford is now open to the public, and among the rooms that are on show are the study where Scott wrote so many of his best-sellers, and the dining room where he died. His extraordinary collection of historical memorabilia, from a lock of Bonnie Prince Charlie's hair to Napoleon's pen case, is also on display.

ABOVE: The John Buchan Centre in Broughton is full of memorabilia connected with the author. The centre was originally the local Free Church in which Buchan's parents were married.

Broughton

BIGGAR, SOUTH LANARKSHIRE

The young John Buchan (1875–1940), who later became a novelist, publisher and politician, spent his school holidays in Biggar at his grandparents' house, The Green. The town held sentimental memories for his parents, who were married at the local Free Church, which is now the John Buchan Centre. Both Buchan and his sister, Anna, found Broughton a source of creative inspiration. For Buchan, it became Woodilee in *Witch Wood* (1927), while Anna, who wrote under the pseudonym O. Douglas, completed her novel *Penny Plain* (1913) while staying here.

John Buchan took inspiration from other areas of Scotland as well for his novels. It is popularly believed that the flight of steps leading up to Ravenscraig Castle in Fife inspired the title of *The Thirty-Nine Steps* (1915), which is the novel for which Buchan is best known. It catapulted him to popular fame, although he would have much preferred to have been known as a serious man of letters. Indeed, he wrote many biographies of important figures, including Sir Walter Scott, but these were eclipsed by his more popular adventure novels, such as *Greenmantle* (1916).

In politics, Buchan received the respect he craved and was Governor General of Canada from 1935 to 1940. When he was awarded a baronetcy, he chose to be known as Baron Tweedsmuir, after the village, where Robert Burns used to drink in The Crook Inn, near Broughton.

Brownsbank

BIGGAR, SOUTH LANARKSHIRE

This tiny cottage was the home of Hugh MacDiarmid (1892–1978), one of Scotland's greatest 20th-century poets, from 1951 until his death in 1978. It was from here that, when he was not travelling the world on lecture tours, he entertained many of the literary visitors who flocked to pay homage to the man credited with leading Scotland's literary and cultural renaissance.

MacDiarmid was the pen name of Christopher Murray Grieve, who was born in Langholm, in Dumfriesshire, in 1892. He developed a political conscience at an early age and in 1928 helped to found the National Party of Scotland, although he was expelled in 1933. A year later he joined the Communist Party, but was expelled from that in 1938.

Grieve began to write under his pseudonym in 1922 and his first collection of poetry, *Sangschaw*, was published in 1925, with a preface by John Buchan.

ABOVE: Hugh MacDiarmid and his wife, Valda, squeezed themselves into this tiny cottage for more than 20 years. His poem, 'The Little White Rose', is engraved by the front door.

A Drunk Man Looks at the Thistle, which is widely considered to be MacDiarmid's greatest work, was published in 1926. In 1931, MacDiarmid launched the leftist sympathies of that decade when he wrote *First Hymn to Lenin*, which acted like a clarion call to poets such as C. Day-Lewis, Stephen Spender and W.H. Auden.

MacDiarmid married his second wife, Valda, in the early 1930s and they lived in Whalsay, in Shetland, from 1933 to 1942. He wrote of his feelings about this part of the world in *The Islands of Scotland* (1939). His autobiography, *Lucky Poet* (1943), was so offensive to some of the inhabitants of his hometown of Langholm that they objected to the idea of him being buried there in 1978, but their opinions were overruled. He is now commemorated on a hill there near Newcastleton, in a large metallic sculpture, which is shaped like a book.

Glasgow

CITY OF GLASGOW

As far as the poet John Betjeman was concerned, Glasgow is 'the greatest Victorian city in the world'. For decades it was considered to be the grimy, rough and poor relation of genteel Edinburgh, with the 'Gorbals Diehards', who appear in some of the novels of John Buchan, forming a stark contrast to the nicely brought up Edinburgh schoolgirls who were described in *The Prime of Miss Jean Brodie* (1961) by Muriel Spark (born 1918). Nevertheless, Glasgow hauled itself up by its bootstraps in the 1980s and dusted off its rough, tough image and it is now enjoying a cultural renaissance.

Glasgow's George Square is dominated by a statue of Sir Walter Scott. Statues of other luminaries, such as Robert Burns, the Glaswegian poet Thomas Campbell (1777–1844) and Queen Victoria herself, are arranged around the base of the plinth. Thomas De Quincey rented rooms at 79 Renfield Street in the 1840s, although he rarely put in an appearance. He would have been the ideal lodger, but for his growing addiction to opium and his tendency to run out of money.

When John Buchan wrote of the Gorbals Diehards he knew what he was talking about, as he and his sister, Anna, grew up in Glasgow and similar boys had attended John's Sunday school. The Buchan family lived in Queen Mary Avenue until the 1890s, and John and Anna were educated at Hutcheson's Grammar School in the city. John then read law at Glasgow University, during which time he compiled an anthology of the essays of Francis Bacon and wrote his first novel, *Sir Quixote of the Moors*.

A.J. Cronin (1896–1981) was another student of Glasgow University. He read medicine and practised as a doctor for some time before putting pen to paper. *The Citadel* (1937) is one of his best known novels, although he is now chiefly remembered as the creator of Dr Finlay of Tannochbrae.

Not every student of the university did well here, or even stayed the course. James Boswell was sent to the university in 1759 by his father, who hoped that it would put paid to his son's unsuitable attachment to an actress. Boswell did not stay long and soon decamped for London, where he was received into the Roman Catholic church. As far as his Calvinist parents were concerned, this was even worse than sleeping with actresses and he was soon persuaded to revert to Protestantism.

Alistair MacLean (1922–87) was born in Glasgow and educated at Hillhead High School. The Second

World War interrupted his formal education and he joined the Royal Navy, but this gave him valuable experience when writing the adventure stories that later made him so famous. After the war MacLean went to Glasgow University and graduated in 1947. He taught English at Gallowflat School in the Rutherglen district of Glasgow and began to write short stories in his spare time.

MacLean's entry into the world of professional writing sounds like a work of fiction in itself because it happened so quickly and smoothly. When one of his short stories won a competition in the *Glasgow Herald*, MacLean was commissioned by the Glasgow publishers, William Collins, to write a novel. He completed *HMS Ulysses* in ten weeks and then watched as it sold over a quarter of a million hardback copies in just six months. In later years MacLean wrote screenplays as well as books, all of which were a success. Many of his books sold over a million copies.

BELOW: Glasgow has long been famous for its writers, but a new generation, spearheaded by Alasdair Gray, James Kelman and Liz Lochhead, is now making a name for itself.

17 Heriot Row

EDINBURGH

In 1857, Thomas and Margaret Stevenson moved with their young son, Robert (1850–94), to 17 Heriot Row, in Edinburgh's New Town. Robert Lewis (later Louis) was born in the city, but perhaps the damp, cold climate disagreed with him because he was a sickly child. He was entertained by his adored nurse, Alison Cunningham, who regaled him with stories about the Scots Presbyterian martyrs, and read to him from the Victorian 'penny-dreadfuls', as the serial novels that were so popular at the time were known. He later immortalized his childhood in such poems as 'The Land of Counterpane' from *A Child's Garden of Verses* (1885).

Stevenson attended Edinburgh University, where he seemed to be more interested in adopting the dress and lifestyle of a Bohemian than in pursuing any form

ABOVE: Thomas De Quincey rented rooms in Glasgow but rarely visited them. He had a hand-to-mouth existence, not helped by his addiction to opium. Despite this, he lived to the age of 74.

ABOVE: The story of Jekyll and Hyde, in which a decent man grapples with his evil alter ego, explores the theme of dualism that fascinated its author, Robert Louis Stevenson.

of study. It was while he was working towards a law degree that he realized he wanted to be a writer, and he began to write essays before branching out into novels. He particularly enjoyed writing about his travels, publishing several books on the subject, including *An Inland Voyage* (1878) and *Travels with a Donkey in the Cevennes* (1879). Stevenson nursed a broken heart while writing the latter book, as he had met and fallen in love with Fanny Osbourne, a married American woman ten years older than him. After she sent Stevenson a cablegram in 1879 breaking off their relationship, he impetuously sailed from Greenock in Scotland to New York, from where he took the train to California in the hope that he might manage to change her mind. The journey nearly killed him, but he survived and turned the experience into several stories.

Under the wide and starry sky
Dig the grave and let me lie…

EPITAPH OF ROBERT LOUIS STEVENSON

Stevenson's persistence eventually persuaded Fanny to divorce her husband, and the couple were married in San Francisco in 1880. Although Stevenson's parents had originally been horrified at their son's involvement with a married woman, they were enchanted by their new daughter-in-law when Stevenson brought her back to 17 Heriot Row in August 1880.

Stevenson was already ill with what is now thought to be tuberculosis, but he managed to write some of his most enduring and popular work after his marriage, including *Treasure Island* (1883), *Kidnapped* (1886) and *The Strange Case of Dr Jekyll and Mr Hyde* (1886). After the death of his father in 1887, Stevenson sailed for the South Seas in the hope of improving his health, accompanied by his wife, his stepson and his mother. They settled in Samoa, where Stevenson wrote several novels, including *The Master of Ballantrae* (1889) and *Catriona* (1893), which was the sequel to *Kidnapped*.

The climate in Samoa and around the equator suited Stevenson, but his heart lay in Scotland. He knew he would never return there, and his longing for his native homeland infused *Weir of Hermiston*, which he was still working on when he died suddenly of a brain haemorrhage in December 1894. As he had requested, he was buried at the top of Mount Vaea in Samoa, and his grave bore some of the words from his poem 'Requiem'.

Milne's Bar

HANOVER STREET, EDINBURGH

This is one of the bars in Edinburgh that is most closely associated with some of the greatest names of Scottish 20th-century poetry; the other two are the Café Royal and the Abbotsford. However, Milne's Bar has such strong connections with the giants of modern Scottish verse that it is popularly known as the Poets' Pub, which is also the title of a painting by Alexander Moffat of seven of these poets sitting together in a venue that is an imaginative amalgam of Milne's Bar, Abbotsford and the Café Royal.

The four names with the greatest links to Milne's Bar are Hugh MacDiarmid, Sorley MacLean (1911–96), Norman MacCaig (1910–96) and Sydney Goodsir Smith (1915–75). MacDiarmid spent many years living at Brownsbank near Biggar (see pages 107–108), and Sorley MacLean is associated with Oskaig where he was born and is buried (see pages 124–5). MacCaig, on the other hand, was an Edinburgh man, having

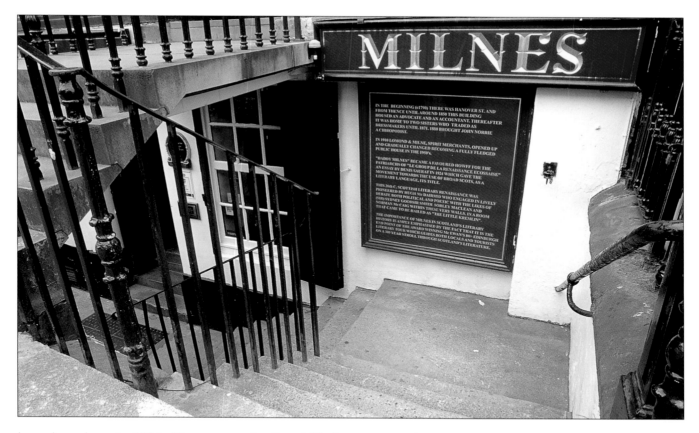

In the beginning (c1790) there was Hanover St. and from thence until around 1850 this building housed an advocate and an accountant. Thereafter it was home to two sisters who traded as dressmakers until 1871. 1880 brought John Norrie a chiropodist.

In 1910 Lomond & Milne, spirit merchants, opened up and gradually changed becoming a fully fledged public house in the 1950's.

"Daddy Milnes" became a favoured howff for the patriarchs of "Le Group de la Renaissance Ecossaise" an essay by Denis Saurat in 1924 which gave the movement towards the use of broad Scots, as a literary language, its title.

This 20th C. Scottish Literary Renaissance was pioneered by Hugh McDairmid who engaged in lively debate both political and poetic with the likes of Ofair Sydney Goodsir Smith Sorley Maclean and Norman McCaig within these very walls. In a room that came to be hailed as "the little Kremlin".

The importance of Milnes in Scotland's literary history is amply emphasised by the fact that it is the end point of the award winning Me Ewan's 80+ Edinburgh literary tour which guides both locals and tourists on a 300 year stroll through Scotland's literature.

been born here in 1910. He went to the Royal High School, followed by Edinburgh University, where he became a Fellow in Creative Writing in 1967. MacCaig's heart also belonged to Assynt, and many of his poems describe the landscape of the North Highlands. Sydney Goodsir Smith was born in New Zealand, but his mother was Scottish and he later immersed himself in the culture, history and language of Scotland, where he lived for most of his life. He wrote his poetry in Scots, and was greatly loved for the romantic, rollicking nature of his work.

The Scott Monument

PRINCES STREET GARDENS, EDINBURGH

The Scott Monument looms over Princes Street Gardens, leaving no doubt about the place that Sir Walter Scott occupied in the collective hearts of Victorian Scotland. He was revered for his novels and poems, which made him immensely wealthy, and also for such patriotic acts as rediscovering the Honours of Scotland, as the Scottish Crown Jewels are called, in a casket in a disused room in Edinburgh Castle.

ABOVE: Milne's Bar has such strong connections with some of the greatest modern Scottish poets that is known as the 'Poets' Pub'. The bar also goes by the nick-name of 'The Little Kremlin'.

Scott died in 1832, and in 1836 a competition was launched to find a suitable design for his monument. A carpenter, George Meikle Kemp, won the competition in 1838 and the foundation stone was laid on 15 August 1840. The Scott Monument was finally opened in August 1846 and has been a big tourist attraction ever since. It was carved from Pale Binney sandstone from West Lothian, and the central sculpture, which depicts Scott accompanied by his deerhound, Maida, was created by Sir John Steell from a block of Carrara marble. The monument is decorated with statuettes of 64 characters from Scott's novels, as well as statuettes of 16 Scottish writers. A copy of Scott's statue stands in Central Park, New York, opposite another of Robert Burns.

Scott is most famous for his series of 'Waverley' novels, after which Edinburgh's main railway station is named, which were a tremendous success when they were first published. In these novels, which included *Waverley* (1814), *Rob Roy* (1817) and *A Legend of Montrose* (1819), Scott's characters were caught up in some of the turbulent events from Scotland's past. The public could not get enough of them, although they must have wondered about the true identity of the author, as Scott published them under the unlikely pseudonym of Jebediah Cleisbotham or 'Author of *Waverley*'. He had several other pseudonyms, including Malachi Malagrowther, Captain Clutterbuck, Lawrence Templeton and Crystal Croftangry. However, his anonymity vanished with the onset of his financial problems in 1825–6 (see pages 106–7), much to the disappointment of some of his devoted readers who knew Scott as a celebrated poet. Apparently Beethoven, when on his deathbed in 1827, threw away the Scott novel he had been reading with the disgusted comment, 'Why, the fellow writes for money!'

The Royal Mile

EDINBURGH

Running from the Palace of Holyroodhouse to Edinburgh Castle, the Royal Mile is actually four streets that form the spine of Edinburgh's

Old Town: Canongate, High Street, Lawnmarket and Castlehill. You can almost smell and taste the history here, helped by the evocative street names and the many old buildings that have survived the sooty, chilly air of Auld Reekie, as Edinburgh is popularly known.

To walk along the Royal Mile is to take a trip back into literary history, as so many famous writers have had associations with it. Daniel Defoe, who lived in the Royal Mile in 1707, described it as 'the largest, longest and finest street… in the World'. Allan Ramsay (1686–1758), the 18th-century poet who started the first circulating library in Scotland, had a bookshop in Niddry's Wynd (now Niddry Street) from 1718 to 1726. While he was here he wrote *The Gentle Shepherd* (1725), the pastoral drama for which he is best known. He later moved to Goose Pie House near the castle esplanade, and there is a statue of him in Princes Street Gardens.

Dr Samuel Johnson made his first trip to Edinburgh in 1773, at the start of his long tour of the Hebrides with his friend and later biographer, James Boswell, and stayed in St Mary's Wynd (now St Mary's Street) off Canongate. Boswell himself lived in James Court, off Lawnmarket, for a while. This house was later destroyed in a fire, and so the only Edinburgh residence of Boswell's to survive is 15A Meadow Place.

Tobias Smollett (1721–71) described Edinburgh and some of its authors in *The Expedition of Humphry Clinker* (1771), after visiting his sister at 182 Canongate in 1766. A plaque on the wall of 22 St John Street commemorates the event.

Thomas De Quincey lived at various addresses in Edinburgh from 1828 until his death in 1859. However, whenever his financial problems became too acute and the attention of his creditors was too pressing, he moved to the Sanctuary in Holyrood, which was a collection of houses that provided a refuge for debtors. It was an escape route that De Quincey became very familiar with.

Brodie's Close

LAWNMARKET, EDINBURGH

Edinburgh has two faces – the sunny, cheerful face typified by the city's annual arts festival and a darker side, characterized by the alleyways or

LEFT: The Scott Monument dominates Princes Street Gardens and is a fitting testament to Sir Walter Scott, many of whom's books educated his readers about Scotland's past.

ABOVE: The Royal Mile runs through Edinburgh's Old Town. Daniel Defoe lived at Mowbray House in the Lower High Street in the early 1700s while working as an English spy.

ABOVE: The brooding atmosphere of Brodie's Close still conjures up images of Deacon Brodie and the sinister nocturnal activities of Robert Louis Stevenson's Dr Jekyll.

wynds that snake off the Royal Mile (see page 112) and which evoke nefarious deeds. This, after all, is the city of Burke and Hare, the notorious 'resurrectionists', as grave-robbers were euphemistically referred to in Victorian times. These two kept the Edinburgh physician, Robert Knox, supplied with a steady flow of dead bodies, many of which the pair had murdered, in the 1820s.

Such stories fascinated the young Robert Louis Stevenson, who was born in the city in 1850. One of his earliest works was *The Body Snatchers* (1881), which was set in Glencorse Old Church, Lothian.

Another sinister tale that intrigued him was that of Deacon William Brodie, the cabinet-maker who was a staunch member of the Town Council by day and a burglar by night. Brodie's Close was named after his father, Francis, and it is where Deacon Brodie lived until he was forced to escape to the Netherlands. He was caught and returned to Edinburgh, where he was hanged. The story of a man with a personality that is torn between good and evil was the essence of *The Strange Case of Dr Jekyll and Mr Hyde*, which Stevenson wrote in 1886.

Edinburgh also features in the contemporary crime novels of Ian Rankin (born 1960), and there are tours tracing the steps of his sleuth, Inspector Rebus.

Lady Stair's House

LAWNMARKET, EDINBURGH

The evocative and atmospheric location of Lady Stair's House is the ideal setting for the Writers' Museum, which commemorates the literary careers of three of Scotland's greatest writers: Robert Burns, Sir Walter Scott and Robert Louis Stevenson.

All three had links with Edinburgh. Robert Burns came to the Scottish capital in the winter of 1786–87, where he was celebrated as the author of the newly published *Poems, Chiefly in the Scottish Dialect* (1786). He was uncomfortable in Edinburgh, thanks to his politics and apparent support for the now lost Jacobite cause, and he could not make enough money from his writing, so he returned to farming in Dumfries (see page 103).

Robert Louis Stevenson was born in Edinburgh. His background was very different from that of Burns because he came from a distinguished family of engineers, against whom he did his best to rebel by visiting brothels while he was at Edinburgh University. Although he initially trained as an engineer, with the intention of following in his father's footsteps, Stevenson soon switched to studying law, before giving it up after he got his degree and becoming a

ABOVE: Lady Stair's House, built in 1622, stands in a narrow alleyway off the Lawnmarket section of the Royal Mile. Robert Burns lodged in Lady Stair's Close during his visit to Edinburgh in 1786.

The High Kirk of St Giles

HIGH STREET, EDINBURGH

This is the parish church of medieval Edinburgh, and it was from here that John Knox (c. 1513–72) orchestrated the Scottish Reformation in the 1550s when he was the minister. He was the author of *First Blast of the Trumpet Against the Monstrous Regiment of Women* (1558), an infamous polemic against Mary, Queen of Scots, which also managed to offend Mary Tudor, Princess Elizabeth who later became Elizabeth I, and Catherine de Medici of France.

Given the strict morals of John Knox and his fellow Calvinists, it is hardly surprising that there was an uproar when a special window dedicated to the memory of Robert Burns was placed in the church in 1985. Burns' life, full of women and alcohol, was in complete contrast to the ideals of Scottish Presbyterianism.

A pattern set in the cobblestones outside the cathedral in the High Street marks the site of an old tollbooth that has long since vanished. It was built in 1466 and finally demolished in 1817, by which time it was a prison known as the Heart of Midlothian. It was the inspiration for Sir Walter Scott's novel of the same name, which was published in 1818. The book begins in the prison and tells the story of Jeanie Dean, who travels to London to appeal on behalf of her sister, who has been wrongly charged with the murder of a child. The novel was based on the true story of Helen Walker, who undertook the same journey for the same reason in the 18th century.

Canongate Kirk

CANONGATE, EDINBURGH

Although he only had a short life, Robert Fergusson (1750–74) had a tremendous impact on the world of Scottish poetry. He was born in Edinburgh, and went to the High School there before progressing to Dundee Grammar School when he was 12 years old. Fergusson became a student of St Andrews university in 1765, but when his father died

professional writer. His health was always frail and he spent much of his life searching for a suitable climate in which to live. His travels took him all over the world, feeding his creative imagination, but Scotland was always his greatest source of inspiration.

Like Stevenson, Sir Walter Scott was born in Edinburgh and had a legal training. Unlike Stevenson, however, he persisted with it and was apprenticed to his father, a solicitor, in 1786 before being called to the bar at the age of 21 in 1792. In 1799 he was appointed Sheriff-Deputy of Selkirk, and in 1806 was also made clerk to the Court of Session in Edinburgh. He now had two jobs, but a chronic shortage of money meant that he had to turn himself into what he described as 'a writing automaton' in order to fund his extravagant, comfortable lifestyle. Such constant pressure, coupled with two severe episodes of financial problems (see pages 106–7), eroded his health and he died in 1832.

two years later he had to return to Edinburgh to look after his mother and sister.

Fergusson started writing poetry while he was at St Andrews. The first poem he is known to have written has the rather unwieldy title of 'Elegy on the Death of Mr David Gregory, Late Professor of Mathematics at the University of St Andrews' (1765). It was notable for its humour and also for being written in the Scots language rather than in English, which was the preferred language of most educated Scots writers of the time.

Once back in Edinburgh, Fergusson combined writing poetry with his job as a clerk in the Commissary Office. He became a contributor to the Edinburgh publication, *The Weekly Magazine*. At first he wrote in English, but he then wrote 'The Daft Days' (1772), which was in the Scots language. Fergusson's first collection of poetry was published in 1773 and had a powerful effect on Robert Burns, who was moved to emulate Fergusson's verse. Burns did so in 'The Cotter's Saturday Night', which was inspired by Fergusson's 'The Farmer's Ingle'.

This early literary promise was snuffed out in 1774 when Fergusson died at the age of 24. He suffered from depression, which was made worse by his drinking. After a fall, he sustained brain damage and was declared 'insensible' and admitted to the local mental asylum. He was buried in Canongate Kirk, in Canongate, and lies under a headstone that was donated by Robert Burns in 1786. Burns also wrote Fergusson's epitaph.

Scottish Poetry Library

EDINBURGH

If you are looking for examples of contemporary Scottish poetry, whether written in English, Scots or Gaelic, this is the place to come. The library is housed in a new building close to the Scottish Parliament, although it has collections at other locations in Scotland as well. There is also a poetry van that travels around the country, which not only has books, cassettes and magazines that can be borrowed, but also hosts writers' workshops, poetry readings and talks.

The Scottish Poetry Library was founded in 1984 and has built up an extensive collection since then. Although its name suggests that it offers only historic and

ABOVE: There are memorials to Robert Louis Stevenson and Robert Burns in the High Kirk of St Giles. Stevenson's is a bronze relief on the south side of the church.
BELOW: The Scottish Poetry Library has an enthralling collection of historic and contemporary poetry, by both Scottish and other writers.

modern Scottish poetry, in fact it contains poetry from around the world as well as verse written specially for children.

Anyone who believes that poetry is a dying art, or that it has no relevance for the contemporary reader, may change their mind once they have visited the library and immersed themselves in the extraordinary legacy that Scottish poetry has given the world.

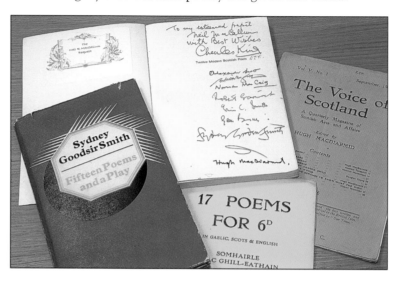

CHAPTER 8

Northern Scotland

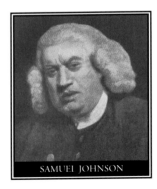

SAMUEL JOHNSON

The Firth of Forth forms a natural border between the northern and southern parts of Scotland, both of which have such different characters and atmospheres. Northern Scotland has a more rugged and wild coastline, and its spectacular rockiness has attracted writers of every ilk. George Orwell chose to spend what turned out to be the last years of his life on the Isle of Jura, and revelled in its remoteness, while Gavin Maxwell enjoyed the final years of his life with his otters at Sandaig overlooking the Isle of Skye. Scotland has a unique literary heritage, which many writers have chosen to protect and continue. Some, like Sir Walter Scott, have done so by collecting Scots poems and ballads, as well as by writing novels that have contributed a vast amount to Scottish culture. Others, such as Sorley MacLean, have done so by choosing to write in Gaelic instead of English.

J.M. BARRIE

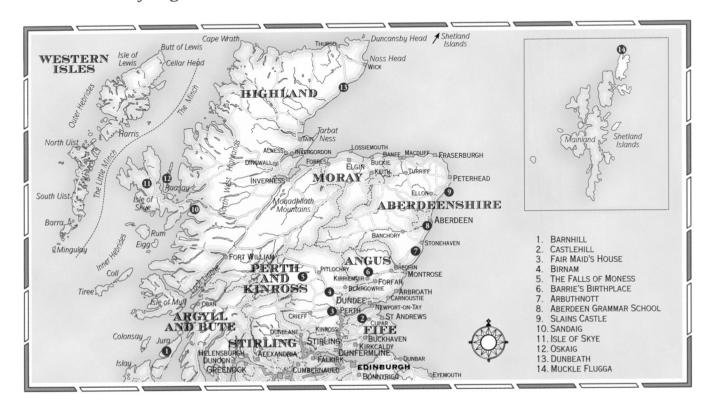

1. BARNHILL
2. CASTLEHILL
3. FAIR MAID'S HOUSE
4. BIRNAM
5. THE FALLS OF MONESS
6. BARRIE'S BIRTHPLACE
7. ARBUTHNOTT
8. ABERDEEN GRAMMAR SCHOOL
9. SLAINS CASTLE
10. SANDAIG
11. ISLE OF SKYE
12. OSKAIG
13. DUNBEATH
14. MUCKLE FLUGGA

Barnhill

ISLE OF JURA, ARGYLL

In 1945 George Orwell visited the Isle of Jura. He was the celebrated author of *Animal Farm* (1945), which was bringing him the first real money he had ever earned, but the pleasure of his literary triumph was overshadowed by his grief at the death of his wife, Eileen, that same year. Her death was made more bitter by the fact that the Orwells had adopted a baby son, Richard, only the year before.

The move to Jura enabled Orwell to concentrate on work as a means of coping with his bereavement. His friends noticed that he seemed ill and emaciated, and shortly after the move he began to show obvious signs of tuberculosis, although he did his best to ignore these. Living in his cottage, Barnhill, was a success and he delighted in exploring the countryside and examining the wildlife. He also began his final novel, *Nineteen Eighty-Four* (1949), while here, although it gave him more trouble than he had anticipated – he referred to it as 'that bloody book'. There were also distractions in the shape of visitors, boat trips and the many delights of summer in the Inner Hebrides.

By the autumn of 1947 his work was also held up by a recurrence of tuberculosis, which led to enforced bed-rest at Barnhill. The novel was finished by the end of 1948 but so was Orwell's stamina, and in January 1949 he took his final journey south to a sanatorium in the Cotswolds, from where he was later moved to University College Hospital, London.

Orwell had done what he saw as his best to escape death from tuberculosis, although he wrote 'Of course I've had it coming to me all my life'. He had remarried in the hope that his wife, Sonia, would prolong his life and had mentally planned several more

books. He had also planned a fishing trip to Switzerland and kept the rods in the corner of his hospital room. However, his lungs could not cope with his disease. As he commented to a friend, 'I've made all this money and now I'm going to die.' He died in hospital in January 1950, five days before his planned trip to Switzerland, and was buried in Sutton Courtenay, Oxfordshire.

Castlehill

CUPAR, FIFE

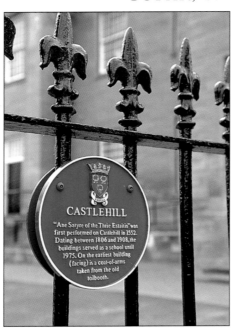

In 1948, a 16th-century Scots play was revived at the Edinburgh Festival, where it has been a popular staple ever since. The play in question is *Ane Pleasant Satyre of the Thrie Estaitis*, which was written by Sir David Lindsay (*c.* 1486–1555) and first performed in 1540. The audience included James V of Scotland, to whom Lindsay was a courtier. It was a morality play that argued for the reform of the Scottish state and church, and which highlighted the venal nature of the 'three estates': the Lords, the Commons and the Church. After the death of James V in 1542, Lindsay had to revise the play somewhat to cope with the vacuum left by the monarch's death. The new version was performed in 1552 on Castlehill in Cupar, where Lindsay lived. By this time, Lindsay had been knighted and given the rank of Lord Lyon King of Arms. He was now in the service of James V's widow, Mary of Guise, who was Regent to her young daughter, Mary, Queen of Scots.

Lindsay died in 1555, but he remained one of the most popular Scottish poets for centuries. His other works included the allegorical poem 'The Dreme' (1528), and *Testament, and Complaynt, of our Soverane Lordis Papyngo* (1538), which contained advice to the king from his parrot.

Fair Maid's House

PERTH, PERTHSHIRE

It is largely thanks to Sir Walter Scott, the aptly named Scottish author, that Scotland's history is celebrated in the way it is today. He effectively launched a one-man revival of Scotland's past, having grown up listening to his grandfather's tales of rough-and-tumble life in the Scottish Borders. These stories fired the small boy's imagination, and although as a young man he embarked upon a career in the law he spent his spare time transcribing old Border ballads. Eventually, Scott moved on to writing historical fiction that covered some of the most vivid eras in Scotland's turbulent past.

When Scott started to write *The Fair Maid of Perth* (1828), he chose a house on the corner of Blackfriars Wynd in Perth as the home of Catherine Glover, his heroine. This is now known as Fair Maid's House, in honour of the book. The novel, a bloodthirsty tale of rivalry in love, was set in late 14th-century Perth and was Scott's final major literary success. After it was published he wrote in his journal 'I can spin a tough yarn still.' Scott continued to write until his death in 1832 but he never again achieved the acclaim he received for *The Fair Maid of Perth*.

ABOVE: Sir Walter Scott chose Fair Maid's House in Perth as the home of Catherine Glover, the heroine of *The Fair Maid of Perth* (1828). It was Scott's last successful novel.

Birnam

PERTHSHIRE

An ancient tree called the Birnam Oak stands behind the Birnam House Hotel. It is popularly believed to be the last survivor of Birnam Wood, which was immortalized by William Shakespeare in *Macbeth*. In the play, the three witches warn Macbeth that his days will be numbered when the wood starts to move. This happens when the army of his enemy, Malcolm, cuts branches from the trees growing in the wood and, while holding them, stealthily advances towards Macbeth's troops. The ensuing battle takes place on Dunsinane Hill, about 15 miles away –

which casts doubt over the authenticity of the Birnam Oak. In 1045, the real Macbeth, who was king of Scotland at the time, defeated a rebel army at Dunkeld, and it is generally believed that this event inspired Shakespeare to write his tragedy.

Beatrix Potter's summer holidays with her family, which were taken in the area around Birnam when she was a child, had a profound impact on her. They were a welcome change after the constraints of life in smoky, grimy London, and she and her brother, Bertram, enjoyed watching and recording the wildlife they found in Scotland. From an early age, Beatrix had a love of natural history that gave her an insatiable interest in everything from spiders to fossils, and a good deal in between. It helped to make up for the loneliness that was the inevitable result of her parents' reluctance to let her have any sort of life of her own, and was the perfect training for her later career as the author and illustrator of children's books about animals.

Each summer while Beatrix was in her teens, the Potter family rented Dalguise House, near Birnam. She loved the countryside, and later wrote 'I remember every stone, every tree, the scent of the heather.' She became friendly with the local naturalist, Charles Macintosh, who shared her fascination with fungi and encouraged her to draw what she found. In 1893, while staying in nearby Dunkeld, Beatrix wrote an illustrated story-letter to the son of her former governess, which formed

the basis of what later became her first children's book, *The Tale of Peter Rabbit* (1902). She was 27 when she wrote the letter and 36 when *Peter Rabbit* was published, and still firmly under the thumb of her parents. Beatrix took the name for the story from that of her own pet rabbit, Peter, who went everywhere with her on his lead. In fact, she based many of the characters in her books on her pets.

Beatrix Potter's connections with Birnam are remembered in the exhibition mounted by the Birnam Institute and in the Beatrix Potter Garden, which recreates many of the characters from her books.

The Falls of Moness

BIRKS OF ABERFELDY, PERTHSHIRE

On 30 August 1787 Robert Burns took one of his favourite walks up the Birks of Aberfeldy. He stopped a short way up the birks and sat on a stone ledge to watch the water from the Falls of Moness tumbling past. The experience inspired him to write a song, called 'The Birks of Aberfeldy'.

The birks was named for the birch trees that grow here and is a woodland walk that runs through a valley near Aberfeldy. The 'crystal streamlet' is the Moness

RIGHT: J.M. Barrie was born in this cottage. Despite being given a baronetcy in 1913 and the Order of Merit in 1922, he chose to be buried in the local Kirriemuir cemetery rather than Westminster Abbey.

OPPOSITE ABOVE & BELOW: Birnam has strong connections with Shakespeare's play *Macbeth*, but it was also a favourite with Beatrix Potter who used to come here on holiday as a teenager.

Burn, which is a tributary of the River Tay. The entire walk, including the stone on which Burns sat – now called Burns' Seat – is clearly marked.

Burns was starting to make a name for himself as a poet at the time of his walk, having published his first volume of poetry, *Poems, Chiefly in the Scottish Dialect*, in 1786. Ironically, he had published the poems partly in order to raise enough money to emigrate to Jamaica so he could escape his personal and financial problems at home. However, the entire print-run of the poems quickly sold out, and Burns decided to stay in Scotland so he could further his literary career. In May 1787, he embarked on what he called 'a slight pilgrimage to the classic scenes of this country [Scotland]', and it was during this pilgrimage that he visited the Falls of Moness.

Barrie's Birthplace

KIRRIEMUIR, ANGUS

On 9 May 1860, James Barrie was born at 9 Brechin Road, Kirriemuir. It was a modest, white-washed cottage and the Barries were a working-class family – his father was a handloom-weaver. Barrie was the ninth of their ten children, and in later years he claimed that his birth coincided with the arrival of some new dining room chairs, which apparently gave his parents more

pleasure and satisfaction than his entrance to the world did. He seemed to be acutely aware of his standing with his parents. He was not his mother's favourite; the sibling who was, David, died in childhood. Barrie did his best to fill the gap that David left, and there are elements of David in Peter Pan, another child who never grew up.

Kirriemuir and Brechin Road strongly influenced Barrie's later writing. In the 1880s, he wrote a short series of novels set in a town called Thrums (a weaving term), which was Kirriemuir under another name. The wash-house at the back of the family home was the model for the house in *Peter Pan* (1904) that the Lost Boys built for Wendy in Never-Never Land.

Arbuthnott

ABERDEENSHIRE

It was while living in Arbuthnott that James Leslie Mitchell (1901–35) wrote his trilogy of novels, collectively called *A Scots Quair* (1946), under the

Now simmer blinks on flowery braes,
And o'er the crystal streamlet plays;
Come, let us spread the lightsome days
In the birks of Aberfeldy.

ROBERT BURNS, 'THE BIRKS OF ABERFELDY'

ABOVE: The Grassic Gibbon Centre, close to Arbuthnott Parish Hall, commemorates the life and work of James Leslie Mitchell and his alter ego, Lewis Grassic Gibbon.

pen name of Lewis Grassic Gibbon. *Sunset Song* (1932), *Cloud Howe* (1933) and *Grey Granite* (1934) told the story of Chris Guthrie, who grew up on her father's farm, was married three times and whose son joined the Communist Party. The novels were rich in Scots dialect and ancient Scots phrases, and celebrated Mitchell's love for his native land.

Mitchell was born at Hillhead of Seggat, where he lived with his crofting family until they moved to Bloomfield in Arbuthnott, in the countryside known as Howe of the Mearns. He later went to Aberdeen and Glasgow, where he worked as a journalist, and then lived in the south of England with his wife. In 1929, he became a professional writer and wrote 17 books in seven years. He adopted the pseudonym of Lewis Grassic Gibbon for his Scots trilogy, and also for *Scottish Scene* (1934), the collection of short stories on which he and the poet, Hugh MacDiarmid, collaborated.

Aberdeen Grammar School

ABERDEEN

It is easy to imagine Lord Byron striding around Greece in his mission to save the country from Turkish rule, or breaking women's hearts left, right and centre. It is less easy to picture him as a small boy called George Noel Gordon and living in Aberdeen with his mother, Catherine Gordon, and his father, Captain John 'Mad Jack' Byron. The family moved here in 1790 when Byron was two, and lodged above a perfume shop. Despite being an heiress, Catherine had virtually no money and her husband was little help as he was rarely present, and when he did put in an appearance it was usually to ask for a loan. 'Mad Jack' died in France in 1791, which left Catherine in an even worse situation, but she managed to find enough money to pay for her son's education, and he attended Aberdeen Grammar School from the age of six. He had been born with a club foot, about which he was extremely sensitive and which would have made him stand out from his fellow schoolboys. It also had an impact on his later behaviour.

Everything changed in 1798 when young George inherited a baronetcy and became the 6th Baron Byron of Rochdale. He and his mother left Aberdeen and moved to Newstead Abbey (see pages 84–5), a virtual wreck that was the ancestral home of the Byron family. Byron was later educated at Harrow and Trinity College, Cambridge, but always said that his love of mountains was born during his childhood in Aberdeen. The city has not forgotten him, either, as there is a statue of him in the gardens of Aberdeen Grammar School.

A later pupil here was Eric Linklater (1899–1974), the novelist born on Orkney who became famous when his satirical novel, *Juan in America*, was published in 1930. He attended the school in the years before the First World War, and was elected Rector of Aberdeen University from 1945 to 1948.

Slains Castle

CRUDEN BAY, ABERDEENSHIRE

Although Slains Castle is now a ruin looking out to sea near Cruden Bay, it was once a perfectly habitable home. In 1773, Dr Johnson and his faithful friend and later biographer, James Boswell, visited the castle and stayed with the Earl and Countess of Errol who then owned it. Both men were on a tour of Scotland, which Johnson wrote about in his *A Journey to the Western Islands of Scotland* (1775). Boswell recorded his own impressions in *Journal of a Tour of the Hebrides* (1785), which was published a year after Johnson's death. In it, Boswell noted that the walls of one of the towers at Slains seemed to extend directly from the rock on which the castle perched.

In the 1890s, Bram Stoker enjoyed visiting this part of Scotland. The craggy scenery fired his imagination and Slains Castle made a particular impression on him. His story, 'Mystery of the Sea', was based on a local ghost story. He started writing his best-known work, *Dracula*, in 1895, and it seems that he had Slains Castle in mind when he wrote about Dracula's castle in Transylvania. There is even evidence that in an early draft of the novel Dracula came ashore at Cruden Bay rather than at Whitby, as in the final version (see page 98).

BELOW: Samuel Johnson and James Boswell were impressed by the dramatic splendour of Slains Castle, which also had a powerful impact on Bram Stoker's imagination.

ABOVE: The city of Aberdeen has not forgotten Lord Byron – there is a statue of him in the grounds of Aberdeen Grammar School which he attended as a child.

Sandaig

GLENELG, HIGHLAND

This is Gavin Maxwell's (1914–69) Camusfearna, where he lived with his otters, Edal, Mijbil and Teko, in a lighthouse keeper's cottage at the edge of the Sound of Sleat. Maxwell came here after an abortive attempt at shark-fishing on Soay off Skye, which he wrote about in his first book, *Harpoon at a Venture* (1952). Sandaig offered the simple life that Maxwell craved, although it changed for ever after he wrote about it in *Ring of Bright Water* (1960). Maxwell called the place Camusfearna rather than by its real name because, he said, such places should remain in the reader's imagination rather than become a reality, but the enchanted readers were determined to travel to see the real thing anyway.

He wrote more books, including *The Rocks Remain* (1963), which was a sequel to *Ring of Bright Water*, and *Raven Seek Thy Brother* (1968). Maxwell's house in Sandaig burnt down in 1968, and his favourite otter, Edal, tragically died in the fire. Maxwell died a year later and his grave is marked by a large boulder placed over the spot where his desk once stood.

In 1963, Maxwell had bought three cottages on Eilean Bàn, a tiny island in the Sound of Sleat, when they were sold by the Northern Lighthouse Board, but he did not move to the island until 1968. His home there is now called the Long Room and can be visited, whereas the island has become a commemorative otter

ABOVE: The sharp teeth of the Cuillin Mountains on Skye have inspired many writers, including Mary Stewart. Those tireless travellers, Boswell and Johnson, visited Skye in 1773.

sanctuary. The Bright Water Visitor Centre, which is dedicated to Maxwell's work, is at Kyleakin on Skye.

Isle of Skye

HIGHLAND

Mary Stewart (born 1916), who has written many popular suspense novels and thrillers, chose the Isle of Skye as the setting for her novel *Wildfire at Midnight* (1956). In it she conjured up the strange atmosphere of the Cuillin Hills. The heroine, Gianetta, is battling with a nervous breakdown when she takes a holiday on Skye, but rather than the rest she was hoping for she has to cope with a killer on the loose and the disturbing presence of her ex-husband.

Life was less eventful for Dr Johnson and James Boswell when they visited Skye during their tour of Scotland in 1773. They stayed on the island for a month, during which time they enjoyed plenty of Scottish hospitality and stayed in some of the best houses. They spent ten days at Dunvegan Castle, where Johnson enjoyed the food immeasurably. When they visited Portree, they dined at McNab's and believed it to be the only inn on the island. One of the most memorable parts of their stay on Skye was meeting Flora Macdonald at Kingsburgh. She gave them a first-hand account of helping Bonnie Prince Charlie to escape to France in 1746, for which she was briefly imprisoned in the Tower of London. Boswell described Flora as 'of a

mild and genteel appearance, mighty soft and well-bred'.

Just after the end of the First World War, a young Sorley MacLean used to catch the ferry from his home on the Isle of Raasay to go to school at Portree on Skye. After training to be a teacher at Edinburgh University and stints as a teacher on Ross and the Isle of Mull, he returned to teach on Skye. He remained a teacher all his working life and wrote the poetry for which he is renowned in his spare time.

A much more recent resident on the island is the Scots poet Kevin MacNeil, who is the inaugural writer in residence for the Highland area of Scotland. His work includes *Love and Zen in the Outer Hebrides* (1998) and *Be Wise Be Otherwise* (2001).

Oskaig

ISLE OF RAASAY, HIGHLAND

Sorley MacLean (or Somhairle MacGill-Eain, to give him his Gaelic name) was born in Oskaig on Raasay in 1911 and returned to the soil of his island birthplace when he was buried here in 1996, next to the grave of one of his daughters. He is acclaimed as one of the great Gaelic poets of the 20th century, and one of the few who helped to rescue the language from oblivion while demonstrating its beauty and subtlety.

MacLean was brought up speaking Gaelic and only started to learn English when he went to school in Portree, on the Isle of Skye (see above), from the age of six. MacLean began to write poetry while he was a student of English literature at the University of Edinburgh, and at first he wrote his poems in English. However, this practice changed in the early 1930s

when he wrote 'The Heron' in Gaelic. He translated it into English, but decided it was far better in Gaelic, and subsequently destroyed all the previous poems he had written in English. By the end of the 1930s, MacLean was widely recognized as an important Gaelic poet, and also as one of the members of the Scottish literary renaissance. However, MacLean chose not to become a full-time poet and after the Second World War, during which he was seriously wounded at El Alamein, he returned to teaching. He was headmaster of Plockton High School from 1956 to 1972. One of his most famous poems is 'Hallaig', which is about a village that was destroyed during the Highland Clearances, but whose long-dead occupants continue to haunt it.

Dunbeath

HIGHLAND

After the Highland Clearances of the 18th and 19th centuries, in which landowners cleared away their tenants to make way for sheep, which were more profitable, Dunbeath was one of the villages created to provide work for the few people who were left. There was a herring boom in 1800, prompting the local landlord to build a harbour for fishing boats, but it did not last.

Neil Gunn (1891–1973), who was born in Dunbeath, explored the themes of the Clearances in his novel *Butcher's Broom* (1934) and of the herring industry in *The Silver Darlings* (1941). He wrote many other books as well and there is a bronze memorial to him by the harbour. Gunn left Dunbeath in 1904 to go to school in Kirkcudbrightshire and study for his Civil Service exams,

ABOVE: Robert Louis Stevenson's visit with his father to see the lighthouse being built at Muckle Flugga on Unst proved very useful when he wrote *Treasure Island* 14 years later.

and later worked at the Glen Mhor distillery in Inverness. At first he combined writing with his day job – he was also an active figure in the Scottish Nationalist Party – but he became a full-time writer after the publication of *Highland River* in 1937. There is information about him in the Dunbeath Heritage Centre and the Clan Gunn Heritage Centre and Museum.

Muckle Flugga

UNST, SHETLAND ISLANDS

Robert Louis Stevenson was born into a celebrated family of engineers; his father, Thomas, designed many of the lighthouses that ring the coast of Scotland. Although the young Robert began to study engineering at Edinburgh University he soon had to tell his father that he would not be following in his footsteps, and instead he turned to the law before finally satisfying his urge to become a writer.

Stevenson often accompanied his father on his trips to the lighthouses that were being built under his instructions, and in 1869 they went to Muckle Flugga, on Unst, to see the work in progress. The lighthouse stands in a dramatic setting, perched on the top of jagged rocks at the northern head of Unst. The island made a big impact on Stevenson and he must have stored his memories of it at the back of his mind because when he came to write *Treasure Island* (1883) the map of the island bore a remarkable resemblance to that of Unst.

CHAPTER 9

Wales

DYLAN THOMAS

Wales may only be a small nation, but it has an enormous literary tradition that stretches back through the centuries and is a source of great pride to its inhabitants. Geoffrey of Monmouth was a 12th-century Welsh historian whose chronicles of royal Britain did much to promote the story of King Arthur, spawning a legend that still captures the imagination today. Some Welsh writers have become so famous that it seems as though the entire culture of their country rests on their shoulders. One of these is Dylan Thomas, who packed an incredible amount of living, drinking and writing into his relatively short life. Whereas another 20th-century Welsh poet, R.S. Thomas, chose to live a very different sort of life on Llyn Peninsula.

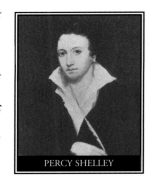

PERCY SHELLEY

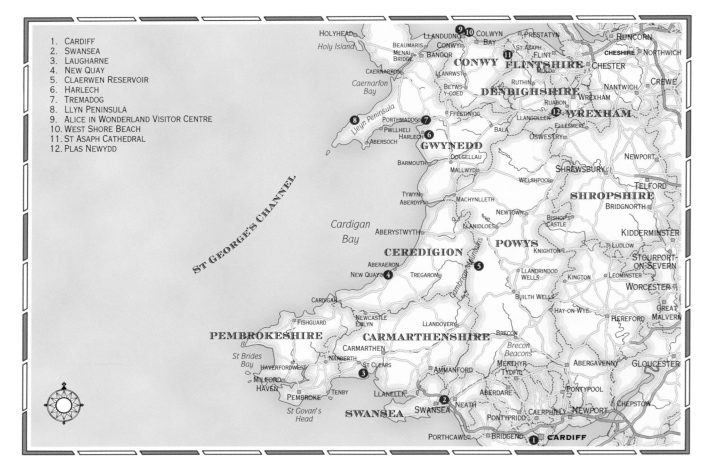

1. CARDIFF
2. SWANSEA
3. LAUGHARNE
4. NEW QUAY
5. CLAERWEN RESERVOIR
6. HARLECH
7. TREMADOG
8. LLYN PENINSULA
9. ALICE IN WONDERLAND VISITOR CENTRE
10. WEST SHORE BEACH
11. ST ASAPH CATHEDRAL
12. PLAS NEWYDD

Cardiff

CARDIFF

The writing career of Roald Dahl (1916–90) effectively began during the Second World War when he fractured his skull in an aeroplane crash. He began to have strange dreams while he was recovering – so weird were they that they inspired him to start putting pen to paper. He wrote *The Gremlins* in 1943, followed by a book of short stories about his exploits in the RAF called *Over to You* (1946). More short stories followed in *Someone Like You* (1953) and *Kiss Kiss* (1959), and in 1961 *James and the Giant Peach* was published in America (it did not appear in Britain for another six years). This marked the start of Dahl's phenomenal career as a writer of stories for children, in which he created a world where children got their own back on dictatorial adults and where virtue was eventually rewarded after many perils. Terrible things happened to horrid adults and nasty children, much to the delight of Dahl's readers, who spanned all ages.

In writing these novels, which included *Charlie and the Chocolate Factory* (1964) and *Matilda* (1988), Dahl was avenging his own difficult schooldays during which his teachers behaved towards their pupils with intolerable and baffling cruelty. Dahl was born to Norwegian parents in Cardiff's leafy suburb of Llandaff in 1916. His early childhood was very happy, but his father and elder sister both died when Roald was three and his mother had to sell her jewellery to pay for his education, first at Llandaff Cathedral School and later at Repton in Derbyshire. He described his childhood and his dislike of his education in *Boy* (1984).

Dahl's father, Harald, had been a partner and co-founder of the ship-broking company Aadnesen & Dahl, so Roald and his sisters were familiar with

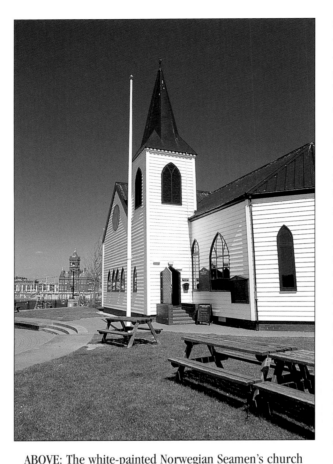

ABOVE: The white-painted Norwegian Seamen's church in Cardiff was rescued and restored with the help of Roald Dahl, who was christened here.
PREVIOUS PAGE: Percy Bysshe Shelley and his young wife, Harriet, were forced to leave Tremadog in 1813 after intruders broke into their house and terrified them.

Cardiff Docks. Fittingly, they were all christened in the Norwegian Seamen's Church there. The 'Little White Church', as it was called, was derelict by the 1980s, and Roald Dahl was the first president of the trust that was set up to restore it, although he died in 1990 before the restoration was complete.

Roald Dahl entertained millions with his short stories and novels, as well as with the television series and films that dramatized his works, so it is entirely appropriate that one of Cardiff's entertainment centres should now be named after him. In 2002, the Oval Basin in Cardiff Docks changed its name to Roald Dahl Plass, in honour of his Norwegian ancestry.

Swansea

SWANSEA

'Land of my fathers. My fathers can keep it.' So said Dylan Thomas, one Wales's most famous poets, whose memory is kept alive in his hometown at the Dylan Thomas Centre. Thomas was born in Swansea on 27 October 1914, at 5 Cwmdonkin Drive in the Uplands part of the city. Much later, he described himself as the 'Verlaine of Cwmdonkin Drive', which was a reference to the fact that the French poet Paul Verlaine (1844–96) wrote most of his poems in the early years of his life, as did Thomas.

In 1925, Thomas went to Swansea Grammar School, where his father was Senior English Master, and in 1931 he became a junior reporter on the *South Wales Daily Post*. Thomas moved to London in 1934 and continued to work as a journalist, as well as branching out into film-making for Strand Films and broadcasting. He quickly became known as a heavy drinker, propping up the bars of Soho (see page 53) and, in the 1950s, of New York. The Welshman had come a long way from Swansea.

Swansea was the home of another man who liked a drink. This was Kingsley Amis, who spent 12 years as a lecturer in English literature at Swansea University from 1949. After starting off in a poky flat, Kingsley and Hilly Amis, and their two sons Philip and Martin (who, like his father, became a novelist), moved to a house very close to Dylan Thomas's old home in Cwmdonkin Drive. It was here that Kingsley Amis launched his writing career with *Lucky Jim* (1954). Amis described his experiences in Swansea in his *Memoirs* (1991), including his encounters with Dylan Thomas, who he described as 'an outstandingly unpleasant man', and his wife, Caitlin (1913–94), as well as with Thomas's last mistress, Elizabeth Reitell. Amis used to drink at the Bryn-y-Mor pub and, long after he had moved away, he retained a strong affection for the city.

Laugharne

CARMARTHENSHIRE

When Dylan Thomas first visited Laugharne in 1934 he thought it was 'the strangest town in Wales'. It was certainly a curious place because it was an English-speaking town that was tucked into an area of South Wales that was predominantly Welsh-speaking. Laugharne was also noted for its eccentric inhabitants.

Thomas loved Laugharne, partly because of the romantic associations it held for him: it was here that he and his wife, Caitlin Macnamara, fell in love in the summer of 1936, having met earlier that year in London. At the

ABOVE & BELOW: Dylan Thomas, loyal customer of Browns Hotel in Laugharne, is remembered in the pub's sign. During the last four years of his life he worked in a tiny wooden shed next to his home, The Boathouse, in the town.

time, Caitlin was in Laugharne with her lover, the artist Augustus John (1878–1961). Thomas and John fought over Caitlin, with the poet the eventual winner. Thomas and Caitlin had run into each other again at Castle House in Laugharne, the home of Richard Hughes (1900–1976), the author of *A High Wind in Jamaica* (1929), who continued to play an important part in their lives.

Thomas and Caitlin were married in 1937 and moved to Laugharne in April 1938. At first, they stayed with Hughes and his wife, but in May they moved to Eros, a fisherman's cottage in Gosport Street, which Hughes had found for them. In August they were on the move again, this time to Sea View in Laugharne. Their first child, Llewelyn, was born in January 1939 and Thomas's book of prose and verse, *A Map of Love*, was published that August. It was a happy, productive time for him, with *Portrait of the Artist as a Young Dog* published in 1940. But money was as tight as ever and in May 1940 the couple had to creep away from Sea View to escape their creditors.

They returned periodically to Laugharne, and in May 1949 they moved to The Boathouse, which is now open to the public. It was bought for them by one of Thomas's patrons, Margaret Taylor, and came complete with a shed in which he could write. By now, Thomas was a celebrated poet, and in 1950 he left Wales for his first tour of the United States. He was still busy writing,

BELOW: One of Dylan Thomas's greatest works was *Under Milk Wood* (1953), which he completed shortly before his death. This portrait of a small Welsh town was filmed in Fishguard in 1971.

although his drinking – he enjoyed visiting most of the pubs in the town, including the Cross House Inn on the Grist and the Three Mariners – and his turbulent private life were distracting.

In the summer of 1951, he completed the first half of his most famous work, *Under Milk Wood*. This recorded 24 hours in the town of Llareggub, which was Laugharne by another name and which, when spelt backwards, described Thomas's changed feelings for the place. Caitlin was also having problems with the town, as she felt suffocated here, especially while her husband was away on his American tours.

Their marriage started to suffer, and in April 1953 Thomas began an affair with a woman called Liz Reitell in America. The première of *Under Milk Wood*, which Thomas narrated, was held in New York the following month. He left Laugharne for his fourth American tour in October. In New York that November, Thomas collapsed and died from complications brought on by his heavy drinking. His body was brought back to Laugharne and buried in St Martin's churchyard, his grave marked by a simple white cross. He was only 39 years old.

New Quay

PEMBROKESHIRE

Dylan Thomas knew this stretch of the Pembrokeshire coast well and was friends with Jack Patrick, the publican of the Black Lion pub

in New Quay. There was nothing unusual about Thomas having friends in the pub trade, as he conducted a life-long love affair with alcohol, even though it did him no good at all and eventually killed him (see page 130). It also distracted him from his work, and his wife, Caitlin, complained that he became 'Instant Dylan' whenever he was drunkenly entertaining his friends in bars.

Thomas was a prolific poet in his youth, concentrating almost three-quarters of his work into a three-year period during the 1930s. In the early 1950s, towards the end of what turned out to be a very short life, he began to experiment with prose, and described the walk along the cliffs of New Quay in *Quite Early One Morning*, which was published posthumously in 1954.

A few miles down the coast, to the south-west, is the town of Fishguard. The Lower Town hugs the harbour and is where the film of *Under Milk Wood*, one of Dylan's best-known works, was filmed in 1971.

Claerwen Reservoir

POWYS

In March 1811, Percy Bysshe Shelley (1792–1822) and his friend T.J. Hogg (1792–1862) were sent down from Oxford for writing and circulating a pamphlet with the inflammatory title *The Necessity of Atheism*. Shelley visited his cousin, Thomas Grove, who lived at Cwn Elan, a house that lies below the Claerwen Reservoir. His young guest found it 'gloomy and desolate', but, despite this, he returned in April 1812 with his

I hold a beast, an angel, and a madman in me.

DYLAN THOMAS

young wife, Harriet. They needed somewhere to live as they were conducting a nomadic existence, travelling from place to place and often relying on the generosity of their friends to provide a roof over their heads.

They stayed at Nant Gwyllt, a house on the west shore of Caben Coch, on the road to the Claerwen Reservoir, until June 1812 when they moved on again. Water played a prominent part in their lives and in their deaths, as Harriet drowned herself in the Serpentine in London's Hyde Park in 1816, and Shelley drowned in a boating accident in Italy in 1822.

The Elan Valley, to which the Claerwen and Caben Coch Reservoirs belong, was part of the landscape in many of the novels of Francis Brett Young (1884–1954). He was strongly influenced by the construction of the reservoirs during his childhood, in which the original bodies of water were diverted from their natural course, and the memories inspired many of his novels, which were set in the Midlands, including *The House Under the Water* (1932). The settings of the novels followed the pipeline of the reservoir 'as beads are threaded on a string'.

BELOW: Scandal was never far away for Percy Bysshe Shelley, and in 1811 he visited his cousin, who lived near the Claerwen Reservoir, after being sent down from Oxford.

Harlech

GWYNEDD

As a small boy, Robert Graves (1895–1985) accompanied his family on their summer trips to Harlech. He grew up in London and had little feeling for the city, but Harlech and Wales were different – he loved them. Graves's father was A.P. Graves (1846–1931), an Irish bard who used to attend the Eisteddfod in Wales and who helped to establish the Welsh Folk Song Society.

Robert Graves and his sister would roam around the hills behind Harlech and, encouraged by their father, they collected the Welsh folk songs sung by the local inhabitants and recorded them on the phonograph they carried with them. Graves was in Harlech on holiday in August 1914 when war was declared on Germany. He immediately enlisted and was given a commission in the Royal Welch Fusiliers. When Graves moved to Majorca in 1929, he chose a place with scenery that was as close to that of Harlech as he could find. This was the year when his autobiography, *Goodbye to All That*, was published. Its matter-of-fact descriptions of the horrors of life in the trenches on the Western Front sent shock waves through Britain.

Graves was entranced by the magic of Wales and, in addition to his poetry, he wrote several books about mythology including *The White Goddess* (1948) and *The Greek Myths* (1955).

Tremadog

GWYNEDD

Local suspicion about the strange ways of incomers is nothing new, and in February 1813 it was played out to dramatic effect at Tremadog. This village was planned and built by W. A. Madocks, who wanted to turn it into a town but was disappointed when this did not happen. One of his plans was to build a causeway that would reclaim some of the land in the Glaslyn estuary. The poet Percy Bysshe Shelley thought it was such a good idea that he offered to help him raise the necessary funds.

In September 1812, Shelley and his 17-year-old wife, Harriet, moved into a house, which has since been demolished, on Madocks's Tan-yr-Allt estate. Here, Shelley wrote a large part of *Queen Mab* (1813), a polemic in which he advocates free love, atheism and vegetarianism among other ideas. The vegetarianism in particular caused problems with the local shepherds, who disliked Shelley's practice of killing any sick or injured sheep that he found while out walking.

Matters finally came to a head one night in February 1813 when intruders burst into the house and shots were fired. Shelley feared for his life. He and Harriet felt they had no choice but to leave, which they did as soon as possible. The culprits have never been identified, but it is generally believed that they disapproved of Shelley's radical political beliefs and wanted to make life as uncomfortable for him as possible.

Shelley always made a point of behaving eccentrically, and another man whose behaviour excited comment – particularly after his death when all sorts of theories were cooked up about him – was T.E. Lawrence, who was born at Woodlands in Tremadog in 1888.

Llyn Peninsula

GYWNEDD

R. S. Thomas (1913–2000) was a poet and priest who spent his life championing the Welsh cause. He spoke out fiercely against what he saw as the horrors of contemporary life, such as its 'awful atheism' and the 'cultural suicide' that was being practised in Wales. Thomas was never afraid to speak his mind, even

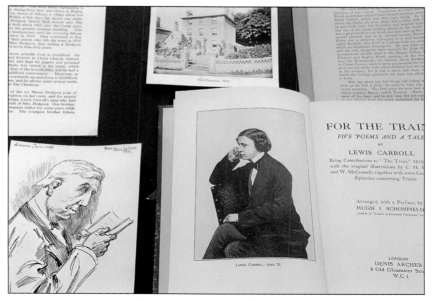

RIGHT: The Alice in Wonderland Visitor Centre in Llandudno displays early editions of Lewis Carroll's books. The Alice books were originally illustrated by Sir John Tenniel.
BELOW: Llyn Peninsula offered R.S. Thomas the perfect refuge in which to write poetry and retreat from other people.

if his views resulted in controversy.

He was born in Cardiff, but his family moved to Holyhead on the Isle of Anglesey when he was five. At first, Thomas spoke only English, but he made a point of learning and speaking Welsh. His autobiography, *Neb*, was written in Welsh in 1985 and was later translated into English, although not by him, and published as *Autobiographies* (1997).

Thomas was a priest of the Church of Wales, and his strong belief in God informed his poetry. He wrote most of the poems in his first three collections of poetry while he was the rector of Manafon, near Welshpool. His poem, 'The Other', is inscribed on slate in the church of St Hywyn, Aberdaron, where he was the priest for 11 years. After spending 40 years as a parish priest, Thomas retired to a stone cottage at Pentrefelin, near Criccieth, where the views of Llyn Peninsula inspired his work and fuelled his passionate belief that Wales should retain its own cultural identity. He died there in 2000, hailed as one of the greatest Welsh poets of the 20th century.

Jan Morris (born 1926) is another famed author who is strongly associated with Llyn. She is a celebrated travel writer who has written about many of the greatest cities in the world, including New York in *The Great Port* (1969) and *Venice* (1960), but who always happily comes home to the village of Llanystumdwy, near Criccieth, where she has lived for over 30 years. Jan wrote about her Welsh home, Trefan Morys, and about Wales – literally the land of her father, as he was Welsh – in *A Writer's House in Wales* (2001).

Alice in Wonderland Visitor Centre

LLANDUDNO, CONWY

Summer visitors to the seaside town of Llandudno may wonder if they have had too much sun when they suddenly come across a large statue of the White Rabbit from *Alice's Adventures in Wonderland* (1865). Rather than being in a permanent bustle because he is late, as he is in the book, this White Rabbit is stationary. It was made from white marble and erected in 1933, when it was unveiled by no less a person than the eminent Welsh politician David Lloyd George (1863–1945).

There are more figures from the book at the Alice in Wonderland Centre, where visitors can find out what it is like to go down the Rabbit Hole and to meet various characters from the book. The characters and the story were invented by the Reverend Charles Lutwidge

ABOVE: The Mad Hatter's Tea Party takes place every day at the Alice in Wonderland Visitor Centre in Llandudno. Hatters often went mad because of the chemicals used in hat production.

Dodgson, and revolved round the adventures of a little girl called Alice. Dodgson, known to us as Lewis Carroll, recounted them to a young friend, Alice Liddell, and the rest of her family before putting them together in a book. Llandudno considers itself to be an important town for fans of *Alice's Adventures in Wonderland* because it is generally believed – although not proved conclusively – that Dodgson stayed here and visited the Liddell family between 1861 and 1864.

West Shore Beach

LLANDUDNO, CONWY

In the 1860s, Henry George Liddell (1811–98), the dean of Christ Church, Oxford, decided to buy a home in Llandudno where he and his wife had spent their honeymoon and several happy summer holidays. They loved the town, and normally resided in a rented house – now St Tudno's Hotel – with their family, but felt the time was right to have a permanent base here. They settled on a house called Pen Morfa on the West Shore. Like their previous Llandudno residence, this has also become a hotel, having been considerably extended over the years and is now called the Pen Morfa Hotel.

Liddell was very well connected, thanks to his elevated position in one of Oxford's most prestigious colleges, and he enjoyed entertaining his friends at Llandudno. Among them were the politician William

Gladstone (1809–98), whose book *Studies on Homer and the Homeric Age* had been published in 1858, and Matthew Arnold, the poet, who also had an interest in Homer. Another frequent guest was one of Liddell's colleagues, the Reverend Charles Lutwidge Dodgson, lecturer of mathematics at Christ Church. Dodgson amused himself, and the daughters of his host, by writing and telling stories about a little girl called Alice, which were published in 1865 as *Alice's Adventures in Wonderland* under the pen name Lewis Carroll.

St Asaph Cathedral

ST ASAPH, DENBIGHSHIRE

This is believed to be the smallest cathedral in Great Britain, and it is certainly a tiny treasure. It was built in the 13th century and was named for St Asaph. He was the successor of St Kentigern, who founded the first church on this site in about AD 560 and was its abbot-bishop. Jocelyn, a monk from Furness Abbey, wrote *The Life of St Kentigern* in about 1180.

In 1152, Geoffrey of Monmouth (c. 1100–1154) was appointed the new bishop of the church of St Asaph. He was a noted historian as well as a priest, and his *Historia Regum Britanniae* (c. 1136) told the story of the kings who lived in Britain from Brutus, who reigned before the birth of Christ, to Cadwallader in AD 689. He also mentioned King Arthur, and in doing so triggered the enormous popularity of the mythic monarch and the legends associated with him. Geoffrey claimed that he got his information from a 'most ancient book in the British tongue', although no trace of such a book has ever been found.

Since then, St Asaph has been connected with another ecclesiastical writer. This is William Morgan (1545–1604), who translated the Bible into Welsh in the late 16th century and was the bishop here. He is buried in the cathedral and there is a monument to him and his fellow translators in the cathedral grounds. Morgan's Welsh Bible had enormous significance, because it preserved the Welsh language, stopped it becoming a mishmash of provincial dialects, and was the inspiration for the books written in Welsh that came after it. In 1620, the Bible was revised by Dr John Davies of Mallwyd and became the standard version.

The Chapter Treasury at St Asaph contains an important collection of Bibles and prayer books, including the first New Testament in Welsh (1587) and Morgan's Welsh Bible (1588).

Plas Newydd

LLANGOLLEN, DENBIGHSHIRE

This is the house of the 'Ladies of Llangollen', two Irish spinsters who caused a sensation when they eloped to Britain together in 1778. They had been close friends – no one knows how close, although there has been much speculation about the precise nature of their relationship – for ten years when they decided to escape from their families across the Irish Sea, dressed in men's clothing and with only one faithful servant to help them. At the time, Lady Eleanor Butler was 39 and the Hon. Sarah Ponsonby was 23. Their families intervened, but the women eventually managed to reach Britain, and the entire episode became the talk of Georgian society.

Eleanor and Sarah came to live at a cottage called Pen-y-Maes, which they renamed Plas Newydd ('New Place') and transformed into a temple to Gothic architecture. They spent almost 50 years here, during which time they prided themselves on improving their minds through culture and read the work of such people as the French philosopher Jean-Jacques Rousseau (1712–78) aloud to one another. As a result, they became a magnet for many noted literary celebrities of their day, including

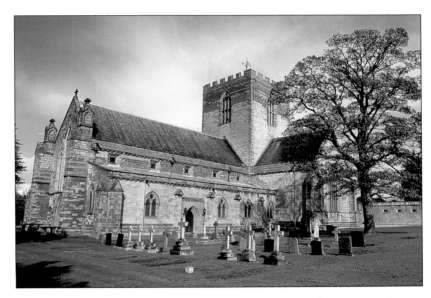

ABOVE: St Asaph Cathedral contains the 19th-century Triglot Dictionary written by Richard Robert Jones, who travelled around Wales with his cat.

Sir Walter Scott, William Wordsworth, Robert Southey, Percy Bysshe Shelley and Lord Byron.

Eleanor died in 1829 and Sarah died two years later, and their house is now open to the public. Their letters, which they always signed jointly, and journals are now considered to be so important that they are held at the National Library of Wales.

BELOW: The 'Ladies of Llangollen', Eleanor and Sarah Ponsonby, lived devotedly at Plas Newydd for almost 50 years.

CHAPTER 10

Ireland

JONATHAN SWIFT

Northern Ireland has had more than its fair share of difficulties, especially with the sectarian violence of the 20th century. Many writers born in Northern Ireland moved over the border to the Republic as soon as they were able, or made for America instead where they were justifiably fêted. Nevertheless, there are some towering names connected with Northern Ireland, including those of Seamus Heaney, Brian Friel and C.S. Lewis.

Thoughts of the Republic of Ireland conjure up images of beautiful countryside, sparkling bays and a more gentle way of life. Dublin is one of the most beautiful cities in the world and is also steeped in literary connections. Who can forget that this is where James Joyce was born and lived until moving to Europe? This is the country of J.M. Synge, Somerville and Ross, Lady Gregory, Samuel Beckett and Patrick Kavanagh, of poets, playwrights, novelists and critics.

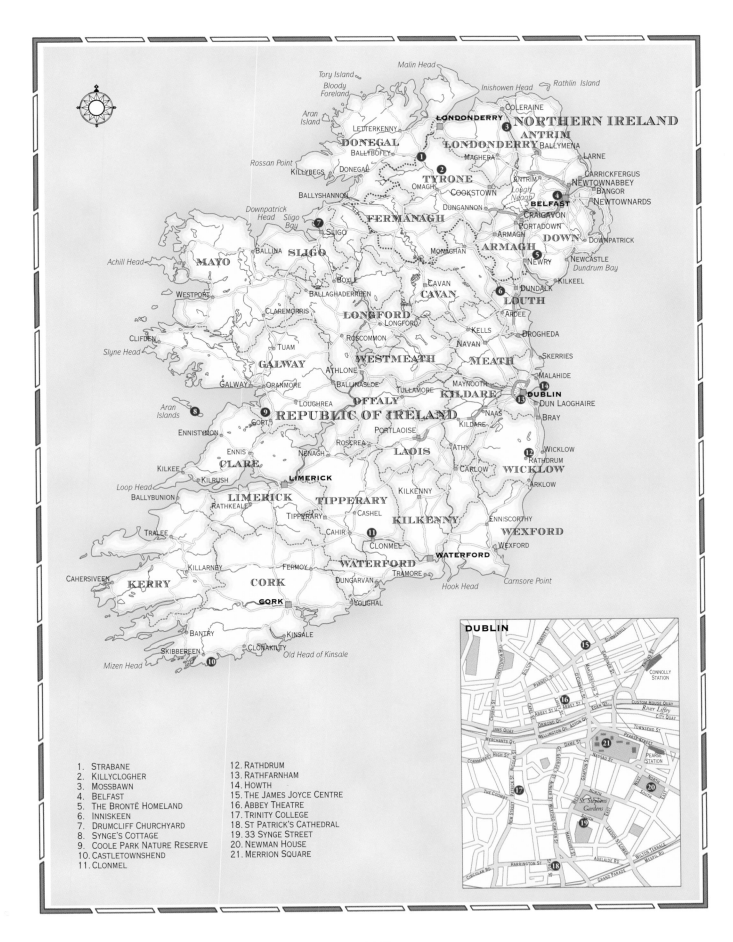

1. STRABANE
2. KILLYCLOGHER
3. MOSSBAWN
4. BELFAST
5. THE BRONTË HOMELAND
6. INNISKEEN
7. DRUMCLIFF CHURCHYARD
8. SYNGE'S COTTAGE
9. COOLE PARK NATURE RESERVE
10. CASTLETOWNSHEND
11. CLONMEL
12. RATHDRUM
13. RATHFARNHAM
14. HOWTH
15. THE JAMES JOYCE CENTRE
16. ABBEY THEATRE
17. TRINITY COLLEGE
18. ST PATRICK'S CATHEDRAL
19. 33 SYNGE STREET
20. NEWMAN HOUSE
21. MERRION SQUARE

ABOVE: In 1911, Brian O'Nolan was born at 15 Bowling Green in Strabane. He grew up to become the writer better known as Flann O'Brien, whose novels were too surreal for their time.

PAGE 136: Trinity College Dublin is the oldest centre of higher education in Ireland, having been founded by Elizabeth I in 1591 as 'the College of the Holy and Undivided Trinity'.

Strabane

CO. TYRONE, NORTHERN IRELAND

Many people, when asked to name an Irish comic writer, immediately think of Flann O'Brien (1911–66), whose surreal flights of fancy continue to amuse and entrance readers. Brian O'Nolan, to give him his real name, was born at 15 Bowling Green, Strabane. His family were Gaelic-speaking and were determined that the young Brian should not mix with anyone who spoke English. Despite his father's best endeavours, which included keeping O'Brien out of school because no decent Gaelic establishments could be found, O'Brien began to speak English after overhearing the forbidden tongue being spoken.

After attending University College, Dublin, the city in which his family now lived, O'Brien joined the civil service. In a ghastly ironic twist, his father died from a stroke on the same day in July 1937 that O'Brien had

passed his exams and been accepted into the civil service, and he found himself having to work to support his mother and ten siblings. It was around this time that he began to write his first novel, *At Swim-Two-Birds* (1939), which concerned a novelist called Dermot Trellis, who was in turn being written about by his own characters. The book was championed by James Joyce (1882–1941) and Graham Greene, among others, but this was no help when it came to getting O'Brien's next novel, *The Third Policeman*, published. It suffered rejection after rejection when it was submitted to publishers in 1939. O'Brien put it to one side in his family home and let it gather dust for the rest of his life. When asked to explain what had happened to it, he often resorted to fibs, such as saying it had been lost on a Dublin bus.

O'Brien always had a close relationship with alcohol and it eventually became so intimate that he was asked to leave the civil service in 1953. It did not help that he wrote a daily column in *The Irish Times* as Myles na Gopaleen, a pseudonym that fooled none of his colleagues. He poured all his creative energy into the column and broke civil service rules, which forbade him to make political statements in public. These columns appeared in book form after O'Brien's death in 1966, as did *The Third Policeman*. This novel has been celebrated as a classic piece of writing ever since.

Killyclogher

CO. TYRONE, NORTHERN IRELAND

When Brian Friel (born 1929) was born in Killyclogher near Omagh, he entered what he later described as 'inbred claustrophobic Ireland'. The country was in the grip of massive political changes and upheavals, all of which influenced Friel when he began his career as a writer. He was also aware of deep divisions within his own family – his grandparents came from County Donegal, were illiterate and only spoke Irish, whereas their son was a teacher.

The contrasts between modern Ulster and traditional Ireland are a recurring theme in Friel's work.

The young Brian went to Long Tower School in Derry, where his father taught, and later attended St Columb's College. He trained to be a teacher at St Joseph's Training College in Belfast, working in the city until 1960. At this point, Friel abandoned his teaching career in order to become a full-time writer of plays and short stories. Some of his stories had already appeared in *The New Yorker* in 1959, and his first play, *This Doubtful Paradise*, had its première the same year, so it seemed to be the right move.

It has been an illustrious career, and Friel is one of the best-known writers in Ireland. His plays have been particularly successful, and have been performed at the Abbey Theatre in Dublin (see pages 150–51), in London's West End and on Broadway in New York. They include *Philadelphia, Here I Come!* (1965), which he wrote after a three-month-long trip to Minneapolis where he worked with the theatre producer Tyrone Guthrie, and *Dancing at Lughnasa* (1990), which later became a successful film.

Brian Friel's life has many similarities with that of his friend, Seamus Heaney (see below), so it seems entirely fitting that in 1980 they helped to found the Field Day Theatre Company, which Friel left in 1990. The first play they performed was *Translations* (1981) by Friel, which was a huge success.

In 1969, Friel and his family left Northern Ireland for County Donegal in the west. His mother came from Glenties and he had spent a lot of time there as a child. Friel later set many of his plays, including *Dancing at Lughnasa*, in a

ABOVE: Brian Friel spent the first ten years of his life in Killyclogher, where he was born. The schisms in his own family, and in Ireland, have informed his writing.

RIGHT: Seamus Heaney, one of the towering figures of contemporary Irish writing, was born at Mossbawn Farm in 1939. He has often written about his family home.

fictional place called Ballybeg, which is based on Glenties.

Mossbawn

TAMNIARN, LONDONDERRY, NORTHERN IRELAND

Seamus Heaney (born 1939), one of Ireland's greatest contemporary poets, was born on his family's cattle farm in Tamniarn. He was the eldest of nine children and later wrote vividly and lyrically of his childhood home, especially in *North* (1975) in which two of the poems are entitled 'Mossbawn'.

ABOVE: In 1966, Seamus Heaney became a lecturer at Queen's University, Belfast, and stayed until 1972. His academic background served him well when he translated *Beowulf* (1999).

Any family hopes that young Seamus might grow up to be a cattle farmer like his father were soon dashed when it became obvious that his destiny lay in a very different direction. He won a scholarship to St Columb's College in Derry, which Brian Friel, his friend and fellow founder of the Field Day Theatre Company, had attended some time before, and became immersed in the academic life.

After attending Queen's University in Belfast (see pages 140–41), Heaney followed the path trodden by so many other poets and became a teacher. In his spare time he wrote poetry, and the awards, prizes and accolades came thick and fast. His first full collection, *Death of a Naturalist* (1966), received rave reviews, as did *Door into the Dark* (1969). However, the sectarian violence of Belfast in the early 1970s made the city an uncomfortable home for Heaney, who is a Catholic, and he and his young family moved to Glanmore in County Wicklow, and later to Dublin.

Heaney's poems show that he has never forgotten growing up in County Down with his family, even during the years when he was teaching at Harvard in America. His mother, Margaret, died in 1984 and *The Haw Lantern* (1987) contains a sequence of sonnets about her. His father, Patrick, died soon after and was remembered in many of the poems in *Seeing Things* (1991).

Heaney's childhood home has not forgotten him, either. There is an exhibition devoted to him at Bellaghy Bawn, the Plantation castle at Bellaghy, including a film of him talking about the impact that the area has had on his poetry.

Belfast

BELFAST, NORTHERN IRELAND

The capital city of Northern Ireland, Belfast was once a city that thrived on shipbuilding and the cloth trade. However, when the Troubles flared up in 1969 it became notorious for bitter and bloody sectarian divisions between Catholics and Protestants. That has changed since the ceasefire of 1994 and the beleaguered city is now rebuilding itself.

Strangely, in a country that prides itself on its rich and influential literary heritage, there are very few monuments to Irish writers in Belfast. One of these rarities is the life-sized statue of C.S. Lewis (1898–1963) outside the Holywood Road Branch Library. It shows him opening the door of a wardrobe, in homage to his world-famous Narnia chronicles, which began with *The Lion, the Witch and the Wardrobe* in 1950. Another library, The Linen Hall Library, has a collection of books that are either by Lewis or about him.

Clive Staples Lewis was born in Strandtown, Belfast, in 1898 and grew up here. He was a strong-minded boy who decided at the age of four that he would henceforth be known as Jacksie – this was shortened to Jacks and finally to Jack. He wrote about his Belfast childhood, including his short spell as a boarder at Campbell College in 1910, in *Surprised by Joy* (1955).

In 1928, the playwright Samuel Beckett (1906–89) spent two terms teaching French at Campbell College before moving on to Paris, where he met James Joyce (1882–1941) and became his secretary. Belfast has always prided itself on its education and its students include Tom Paulin (born 1949), the poet, playwright and critic, who went to Annadale Grammar School, and Seamus Heaney, who began at Queen's University in 1957.

Heaney graduated from Queen's in 1961 and trained as a teacher at St Joseph's College, where he later taught. He then returned to his old university as a lecturer in 1966 and stayed there until 1972 when he left for County Wicklow. It was while teaching in Belfast that Heaney met Philip Hobsbaum (born 1932), the poet and critic, who encouraged him and other young poets, including Derek Mahon (born 1941) and Michael Longley (born 1939). In 1965, Heaney's first collection of poems was published in a pamphlet called *Eleven Poems*. His first collection in book form, *Death of a Naturalist*, was published in 1966 and won several important literary prizes. It was the start of an illustrious career in which one of the highest points was receiving the Nobel Prize for Literature in 1995.

BELOW: Patrick Brontë, father of Branwell, Charlotte, Emily and Anne, was born and brought up in what is now called the Brontë Homeland, near Drumballyroney.

The Brontë Homeland

DRUMBALLYRONEY, CO. DOWN, NORTHERN IRELAND

As its name suggests, this is where the Brontë family had its roots, as it is where Patrick Brontë (1777–1861), the father of Branwell, Charlotte, Emily and Anne, was born and grew up with his parents, before leaving to study theology at Cambridge University.

Patrick was born into a farming family in the village of Emdale on St Patrick's Day 1777, hence his name, but he had no desire to follow in his father's choice of career. Instead, Patrick crammed knowledge into his head at every available opportunity and, helped by the local rector, managed to win a prized place at Cambridge. Patrick returned to Ireland in 1806 and preached his first sermon at the church in nearby Drumballyroney, but he had not come back to stay.

In 1810, he departed for Yorkshire, where he later married Maria Branwell and became Perpetual Curate of Haworth in 1820. They had six children, two of whom died in childhood. The other four achieved almost iconic status as the creative and literary products of a difficult home life and the trials of being separated from one another. Charlotte was the only one who married; she chose her father's Irish curate, the Reverend Arthur Bell Nicholls, who was brought up in Banagher, Offaly, and who eventually returned there after Charlotte's death.

ABOVE: The Patrick Kavanagh Rural and Literary Resource Centre in Inniskeen celebrates the work of one of Ireland's most gifted poets. Kavanagh was born in Inniskeen and his father was a farmer.

BELOW: Ben Bulben occupied such an importance place in the heart of W.B. Yeats that he insisted on being buried near it. One of his last poems was called 'Under Ben Bulben'.

Inniskeen

CO. MONAGHAN, EIRE

Claimed by many to be Ireland's greatest poet after W.B. Yeats, Patrick Kavanagh (1904–67) was born in Inniskeen. Signposts indicate the house where he lived, although it is privately owned and not open to the public. However, the Patrick Kavanagh Rural and Literary Resource Centre, formerly St Mary's Roman Catholic Church, which Kavanagh attended and wrote about in *Tarry Flynn* (1948), is full of information about the man and his work, and occasionally runs writers' weekend courses.

Kavanagh spent his early years as a farmer, but he yearned to become part of the literary world and left his hometown to become a journalist in Dublin in 1931. He wrote from the heart about what he knew, so his poetry concerns the landscape of County Monaghan and the lives of its inhabitants. He was particularly interested in the contrast between the popular view of 'Oirish' life and its realities. Kavanagh's first collection of poetry, *Ploughman and Other Poems*, was published in 1936 and attracted the attention of John Betjeman, although his poetry did not really take off until the 1940s.

Kavanagh is probably best known for his epic poem, *The Great Hunger* (1942), which linked the bleak landscapes in some parts of the Irish countryside with the sexual repression that he felt made people emotionally barren. There was such outrage when the poem was published that Kavanagh was even questioned by the police about its supposed obscenity,

much to his disgust. His other works of both prose and poetry included *The Green Fool* (1938), *Collected Poems* (1964) and *Self Portrait* (1964).

In the 1950s and 1960s, Kavanagh lived in a flat in Pembroke Road in Dublin. He died in the city in November 1967 but was buried in Inniskeen. His friends followed his wishes and erected a simple memorial seat to him by the side of the Grand Canal at Baggot Street Bridge in Dublin. There is a life-size bronze statue of him sitting on a bench on the other side of the canal.

Drumcliff Churchyard

CO. SLIGO, EIRE

In many circles, W.B. Yeats (1865–1939) has been ridiculed for his beliefs in reincarnation, astrology and mysticism, so there is something very touching about the simple headstone on his grave at Drumcliff. It bears, at his request, the final lines from one of his last poems, 'Under Ben Bulben'.

Ben Bulben is the mountain that Yeats loved so much. It overlooks Drumcliff, where his grandfather was rector and where he wanted to be buried. Before his death, Yeats made sure that the epitaph on his headstone and his burial arrangements were exactly the way he wanted them. This irritated his sister, who said he had broken the family tradition of not having a tombstone.

Yeats died in January 1939 at Roquebrune in France, where his body was temporarily buried until

*Cast a cold Eye
On Life, on Death
Horseman, pass by!*

EPITAPH OF W.B. YEATS

it could be transported back to Ireland. Such was Yeats's stature as an Irish poet that the French government offered to carry his coffin home on a destroyer. The Dean of St Patrick's Cathedral in Dublin suggested that he should be buried there (see pages 152–3), but his family preferred to abide by Yeats's wishes and bury him at Drumcliff. However, the start of the Second World War meant that this burial did not take place until September 1948, when it was attended by members of the Irish government among many other mourners.

Synge's Cottage

DÚN CONCHÚIR, INISHMAAN, ARAN ISLANDS, EIRE

WB. Yeats and J.M. Synge (1871–1909) first met each other in Paris in December 1896. Yeats had already established a reputation for himself as a noted poet, playwright and collector of Irish legends, and he had recently visited the Aran Islands, off Galway Bay, on a fishing trip. Synge, on the

MacDonagh family. The cottage has now been turned into a small museum. He enjoyed sitting on the cliffs overlooking Gregory's Sound, tucked into a small, dry-stone shelter that he built himself and which is now known as Synge's Chair.

The visits paid off because Synge wrote a play, *Riders to the Sea* (1905), which was set in Inishmaan and was performed at the Abbey Theatre in Dublin, where Synge became a director in 1906. He followed this with a non-fiction book about Irish peasant life entitled *The Aran Islands* (1907). Synge was also writing other plays, but he was ill and died from Hodgkin's disease in March 1909. Yeats and his patron-collaborator, Lady Gregory, were left with the task of sorting through Synge's manuscripts. Yeats later

other hand, had recently abandoned his musical training in the hope of becoming a professional writer. Yeats, as the author of *Fairy and Folk Tales of the Irish Peasantry* (1888) and *The Celtic Twilight* (1893), suggested that Synge should visit the Aran Islands to see if inspiration would strike.

Synge made several visits to Inishmaan (the middle of the three Aran Islands) between 1898 and 1902, staying for weeks at a time in the summer or autumn. On each occasion he stayed in a whitewashed cottage near Dún Conchúir that was owned by the

wrote about some of the ideas that were triggered by Synge's death in *The Death of Synge and Other Passages from an Old Diary* (1928).

ABOVE: Yeats's emotional life was highly complicated, even after he married Georgiana Hyde-Lees in 1917. He once said 'those who create have to cultivate the wild beast in themselves'.

BELOW: 'My home for nearly 40 years' is how W.B. Yeats described Coole Park, which was owned by his patron and collaborator, Lady Gregory. It is now a nature reserve.

Coole Park Nature Reserve

CO. GALWAY, EIRE

A few walls, a stableyard and a huge copper beech known as the 'autograph tree' – because it was autographed by many famous people – are all that remain of Coole Park. It was once the home of Lady Gregory (1852–1932), the playwright and co-founder of the Abbey Theatre in Dublin (see pages 150–51). Nevertheless, there is a visitor centre to fill in the gaps, with exhibits on Coole and its owner.

In 1896, Lady Gregory met W.B. Yeats, inviting him to Coole Park for the first time the following year. Yeats later described Coole as 'my home for nearly 40 years'. He was recovering from a broken affair with Olivia Shakespear (although they remained close friends for the rest of their lives) and the visit was a great success. Yeats and Lady Gregory began to collaborate on books and plays, as well as planning the Irish Literary Theatre, which led on to them setting up the Abbey Theatre in Dublin in 1904.

Lady Gregory was also helpful to Yeats because she gave him the money that enabled him to give up journalism and concentrate on creative writing instead. They continued to have a fruitful and happy friendship until Lady Gregory died at Coole in April 1932. Yeats spent most of the final year of her life staying with her at Coole Park so she was not alone. She was quite infirm by this time, as he noted in his poem 'Coole Park and Ballylee, 1931'. After her death Yeats wrote some prose called 'The Death of Lady Gregory', which he did not publish, although it has since appeared in *Lady Gregory's Journals II* (1987). Yeats himself died in 1939 and, given his strong belief in reincarnation and the afterlife, was doubtless looking forward to a reunion with his old friend.

Castletownshend

CO. CORK, EIRE

D ean Jonathan Swift (1667–1745) visited the village of Castletownshend when he stayed nearby at Unionhall in 1723, rowing himself over from Glandore Harbour. He was dean of St Patrick's Cathedral in Dublin at the time, but had taken a few months off while he recovered from the

ABOVE: United in death as in life, Violet Martin and Edith Somerville lie next to each other in St Barrahane churchyard. After Violet died, Edith gave an altar to the church in her memory.

death of his close friend, Vanessa. According to the records of the Somerville family, who lived in Castletownshend, Swift wrote his poem 'Carberiae Rupes' in the ruined tower near the harbour.

The Somervilles were still living in their family home, Drishane, in the following century, when Edith Oenone Somerville (1858–1949) started writing books with her cousin, Violet Martin (1862–1915). This was the beginning of a highly successful collaboration between the two women, although they did not write under their own names. *An Irish Cousin* (1889), which was their first work of fiction, was published under the names of Giles Herring and Martin Ross, although they later wrote as Somerville and Ross.

They are best known for two books that described the lives of the Irish gentry and their love of fox-hunting: *Some Experiences of an Irish R.M.* (1899) and *Further Experiences of an Irish R.M.* (1908). Edith had

ABOVE: Each year the Synge Summer School is held in
Rathdrum, in honour of J.M. Synge. His writing life was cut
short by Hodgkin's disease and he died in Dublin in 1909.

been injured in a duel. The family did not stay in
Clonmel long, and Sterne was later educated at
Halifax Grammar School in Yorkshire before
going on to Jesus College, Cambridge.

Sterne is best remembered for his comic
novel, *Tristram Shandy*, and for having a sense
of humour that many found at odds with his
calling as a vicar. He would probably have been
amused by what happened to his body after his
death in 1768. Grave-robbers stole his corpse
from its grave in Hyde Park Place, London,
and sold it. It was recognized when it appeared
at a lecture at Cambridge University, and was
duly reburied.

Anthony Trollope also spent some time in
Clonmel, lodging in Anne Street from 1844 to
1845. At the time he was working for the Post
Office as an inspector of the rural districts of
south-west Ireland. His mother, Frances, wrote
40 novels, and Trollope inherited her industry
and discipline. He got up early each morning
before going to work so he could write a set
number of words. Trollope's first novel, *The
Macdermots of Ballycloran*, was published in 1847.
By the time he died in 1882 he had written 47
novels, plus biographies, travel books and
collections of short stories.

first-hand knowledge of such matters, as she became
Master of Hounds in 1903. Violet also enjoyed riding,
but she had to stop in 1898 after a serious riding
accident. After Violet died in 1915, Edith continued to
keep in contact with her through spiritualism until her
own death at Tally House in Castletownshend in 1949.

Violet and Edith are buried side by side in the
churchyard of St Barrahane in the village. The interior
of the church contains memorials to both women.

Clonmel

CO. TIPPERARY, EIRE

Laurence Sterne was born in this pretty and
ancient town in November 1713. Tradition has it
that he made his entry into the world in Mary
Street (previously known as Our Lady's Street) while
his father's regiment was stationed here. His father
came from Yorkshire, had little money and had once

Rathdrum

CO. WICKLOW, EIRE

John Millington Synge came to writing relatively late,
having first trained as a musician before he realized
that he wanted to be an author instead. In 1896,
W.B. Yeats encouraged Synge to visit the Aran Islands
in search of atmosphere and inspiration, and these visits
proved very stimulating (see pages 143–4). Synge's first
play, *In the Shadow of the Glen*, was performed in 1903. It
was followed by *Riders to the Sea* (1905), *The Well of the
Saints* (1905) and, most notably, *The Playboy of the
Western World*, which caused controversy, sensation and
rioting when it was first performed at the Abbey Theatre
(see pages 150–51) in 1907.

Synge died in 1909 at the age of 38, but the impact
of his writing and his influence as one of the practi-
tioners of Irish Modernism lives on. Each year since its
inception in 1991, the Synge Summer School has met
in Rathdrum to examine the living tradition of Irish
theatre. It offers an impressive array of guest speakers,
as well as theatre workshops.

ABOVE: Rathfarnham Castle is close to Willbrook, where W.B. Yeats spent the last years of his life in a house called Riversdale. Although he was ill, he was still working hard.

Rathfarnham

CO. DUBLIN, EIRE

After the death in 1932 of Lady Gregory, who was a great friend, supporter and collaborator of W.B. Yeats, the poet and playwright wanted to find another house that would bring him the peace he had enjoyed for so long at her home, Coole Park (see page 145). It was not long in coming. In May 1932, Yeats took a lease on a house called Riversdale at Willbrook, just outside Rathfarnham on the south side of Dublin.

It was a barren time for him creatively, caused by a combination of his own ill health and Lady Gregory's death. Yeats had spent much of his life experimenting with psychic matters, including trying to visit his great love, Maud Gonne, on the astral plane, so he experienced intellectual curiosity more than anything else when he began to see apparitions at Rathfarnham. A couple of years after Yeats moved in, he saw a child's

hand holding a playing card that was either the five of hearts or of diamonds, and wondered whether it meant he had five months or five years to live. As it turned out, it was five years.

Although Yeats's life was coming to a close he was still busy writing, and in 1936 he worked on a translation of the *Upanishads* (1937) and revisions of *A Vision* (1937) at Riversdale. In between these bouts of work he enjoyed being pushed in a wheelchair to Rathfarnham and back. Despite Yeats's ill health, he spent a lot of time travelling to France or visiting friends in England. When he died in January 1939, he was in Roquebrune in France, and was correcting proofs until two days before his death.

Howth

CO. DUBLIN, EIRE

The strange tale of Erskine Childers (1870–1922) has as much excitement as *The Riddle of the Sands* (1903), the novel for which Childers is most famous. The book tells the story of two amateur yachtsmen, Davies and Carruthers, who become amateur spies when they discover German plans for the invasion of England. Childers wrote the book as a warning to the British government and people about the dangers that he believed were lying in wait from across the English Channel, but his message counted for nothing and instead the novel was applauded as a wonderful adventure story.

Childers was born in Dublin and grew up in Glendalough, County Wicklow, before moving to England and working as Committee Clerk of the House of Commons from 1894 to 1910. Childers served in the RNAS during the First World War, ending up as a major in the RAF, and then became openly embroiled in Irish politics by joining Sinn Féin and moving to Dublin.

His knowledge of boats and the sea, which he put to such good use in *The Riddle of the Sands*, became vital information in 1914 when Childers became involved in gun-running for the Irish Volunteers. First he bought 1,500 second-hand Mauser rifles in Hamburg while everyone thought he was in Mexico, and then he sailed out to the Goodwin Sands in the North Sea in his boat, *Asgard* (a wedding present from his parents-in-law), to meet the tug bringing the rifles from Germany. He took them on board and

ABOVE: The James Joyce Centre is a Mecca for all lovers of Joyce. Here, they can immerse themselves in many pieces of memorabilia, including Leonard Bloom's original front door.

brought them ashore at Howth.

Childers' change of allegiance meant that he was viewed as a traitor by the British government. He had no option but to go on the run, but he was eventually caught and arrested in Glendalough. He did not contest his arrest and was executed by firing squad in November 1922. With characteristic courage, Childers refused a blindfold and shook hands with each member of the squad, saying to them 'Take a step or two forward, lads. It will be easier that way.'

Howth has another, although much more gentle, literary connection. It was the home from 1880 to 1904 of the Yeats family, who came here from London in the hope of reducing their expenses. Willie, as W.B. Yeats was known to his family and friends, was 15 at the time. The family were lent Balscadden Cottage, which faced north, and they later moved to Island Cottage near Howth harbour. Although they all enjoyed living here, their chronic lack of money meant they had to move back to Dublin in 1884.

BELOW: One of Ireland's earliest literary treasures, now in the library at Trinity College Dublin, is the *Garland of Howth*, which was found on a small island north of Howth Head.

The James Joyce Centre

35 NORTH GREAT GEORGE'S STREET, DUBLIN, EIRE

Although James Joyce spent the greater part of his life in Europe, he is indelibly linked with his home city of Dublin. How could he not be when his most famous novel, *Ulysses* (1922, Paris; 1936,

ABOVE: The Ha'penny Bridge is one of the visual landmarks of Dublin, but the city also takes pride in its many literary connections, no matter how ancient or contemporary they are.

England), describes a single day, 16 June 1904, in the life of the city. Joyce chose the day in question because it was the date on which he and Nora Barnacle, who later became his wife, walked around the city together shortly after first meeting. It is now annually celebrated as 'Bloomsday' after Leonard Bloom, one of the book's three main characters. There are special tours of Dublin that point out all the places that appear in the book,

ABOVE: The Abbey Theatre's first season ran from 27 December 1904 to 3 January 1905. The theatre has weathered many controversies and riots since then but remains a Dublin institution.

such as the Martello tower at Sandycove, which appears in the opening chapters, and 7 Eccles Street, Dublin, which is where Leonard Bloom lived and is marked by a plaque. The original front door of this house is now contained in the James Joyce Centre, which has many other pieces of Joyce memorabilia as well.

Joyce was born at 41 Brighton Square West, in the Rathgar district of Dublin, in February 1882. The family moved around a great deal during Joyce's childhood and adolescence, and their homes included 1 Martello Terrace, Bray; 14 Fitzgibbon Street, Dublin; and 13 North Richmond Street, Dublin. Joyce wrote from an early age and was particularly influenced by W.B. Yeats and the Norwegian playwright Henrik Ibsen (1828–1906). He had already visited Paris twice when he met Nora Barnacle in June 1904, and he took her there in November of the same year. Apart from brief return visits, Joyce never lived in Ireland again. He died in Zurich in January 1941 and was buried in Fluntern Cemetery there.

When Joyce met Nora, he was working on the short stories that were eventually published in 1914 as *Dubliners*. He was offered a publishing contract for the book in 1906. However, the offer was withdrawn in the same year after a disagreement about its bad language – it contained the word 'bloody' – and soon it seemed that no other publishers wanted to touch it, either. This was an experience that became all too familiar for Joyce, especially over *Ulysses*, which was widely condemned as being obscene and was banned in America in 1933 before being published there in 1934. *Ulysses* was not published in Joyce's own country until the 1960s because it was considered to be pornographic.

Finnegan's Wake was published in 1939 and, in tandem with *Ulysses*, was seen as a revolutionary breakthrough in the form and structure of the novel. Joyce had taken the 'stream of consciousness' style pioneered by Virginia Woolf and the French writer Marcel Proust (1871–1922), among others, to a new level. Some readers found Joyce impenetrable, others regarded him as a genius, a debate that continues to rage.

Abbey Theatre

ABBEY STREET LOWER, DUBLIN, EIRE

The first Abbey Theatre opened in December 1904 and was founded by W.B. Yeats and Lady Gregory, the playwright and director. It burnt down in a fire in 1951 but its purpose of supporting Irish theatre lives on in the replacement theatre, which opened in July 1966, even if the building itself is considered to be an eyesore.

The original Abbey Theatre was paid for by Annie Horniman (1860–1937), who had been a member of the mystical Order of the Golden Dawn when Yeats also belonged to it. She enjoyed being his benefactress and supported his desire to create a permanent theatre for the Fays' National Theatre Company, which had been producing his plays. It seems that her good intentions towards Yeats were not confined to helping his artistic output, as she would have liked to marry him and, as a result, was distinctly hostile towards the many women who always surrounded him. Lady Gregory, who became the legal patentee of the theatre, as this position had to be held by someone who was Irish (Annie Horniman came from Manchester), was particularly unpopular with Annie, and Yeats had to tie himself in knots trying to keep both women happy.

One of the buildings that was knocked down to make way for the Abbey had once been a morgue, and during construction the builders found some human remains. They feared they had stumbled across a murder until the caretaker told them that the morgue had once lost a body and this, presumably, was it.

The first plays to be performed at the Abbey were Yeats's *On Baile's Strand* and *Cathleen ni Houlihan*, and Lady Gregory's comedy, *Spreading the News*. The company went professional in 1906, with Yeats, Lady Gregory and J.M. Synge as the three directors. In 1907, Synge's play, *The Playboy of the Western World*, was premiered at the Abbey and sparked riots because many believed it insulted the inhabitants of the west of Ireland. There was more controversy in 1910 when the Abbey performed George Bernard Shaw's *The Shewing-up of Blanco Posnet*.

In 1925, the Abbey became the first English-speaking state-subsidized theatre when it was given a grant from the government of Eire, which enabled it to continue its tradition of showcasing the best of the Irish playwrights. Among those whose work has been performed here are Padraic Colum (1881–1972); Lennox Robinson (1886–1958), who became the Abbey's manager in 1910, its director in 1923 and who later wrote a book about the theatre; Sean O'Casey, whose play *The Plough and the Stars* caused nationalist riots when it was first performed in 1926; and Brian Friel, whose *The Enemy Within*, which is based on the exile of St Columba, was first performed at the Abbey in 1962.

The Peacock Theatre, a small theatre within the Abbey building, mostly concentrates on presenting new plays. These have included *Beauty in a Broken Place* (2004) by Colm Tóibín (born 1955). This is his first play and it is fitting that it should be performed at

ABOVE: *Book of Kells*, an illuminated 9th-century Latin manuscript of the four gospels that was produced in the town of Kells, County Meath, is now on display in Trinity College.

the Abbey because he is the author of a biography of Lady Gregory, *Lady Gregory's Toothbrush* (2002). The title comes from Lady Gregory's comment that the riots caused by Synge's *Playboy* in 1910 were fought between those who used a toothbrush and those who did not.

Trinity College

WESTMORELAND STREET, DUBLIN, EIRE

Some universities seem to act as magnets for students who go on to become famous, and Dublin's Trinity College is certainly one of them. Religion affects many areas of Irish life, and Trinity was only open to Protestants until 1793. Catholic students went to University College, where the poet Gerard Manley Hopkins (1844–89) taught Classics in the 1880s, and whose students have included James Joyce.

Jonathan Swift became a student of Trinity College

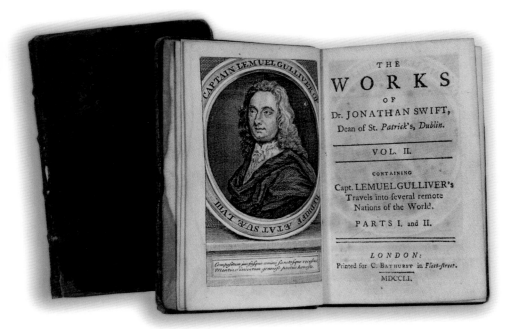

in 1682, but he was later found guilty of creating a disturbance – something which came easily to him, given the political and satirical pamphlets he later wrote – and had to beg the dean for forgiveness on bended knee. One of Swift's fellow students and an old school friend was William Congreve (1670–1729), who is best remembered for his plays *Love for Love* (1695) and *The Way of the World* (1700).

Oliver Goldsmith was a student here in the 1740s and later wrote the novel *The Vicar of Wakefield* (1766) and the play *She Stoops to Conquer* (1773) – a statue of him stands outside the university. Bram Stoker, who spent most of his early childhood ill in bed, distinguished himself at Trinity in the 1860s by winning the University Athletics Championship. He later made himself world-famous by writing *Dracula* (1897).

J.M. Synge, who shocked theatre audiences with *The Playboy of the Western World* (1907), came here in 1889. Samuel Beckett is another playwright who was a Trinity man. His play *Waiting for Godot* caused a sensation when it was first performed in Paris in 1953.

A very important work associated with Trinity College is the *Book of Kells*, which is held in the Old Library. This was written and illustrated in about AD 800 at the monastery on Iona in Scotland, and consists of the four gospels of the New Testament in Latin. The Library also contains the Book of Durrow, which is the earliest known Irish illustrated manuscript, dating from between AD 650–80.

ABOVE & BELOW: *Gulliver's Travels* (1726) by Jonathan Swift, Dean of St Patrick's Cathedral (below), was a satirical attack on the politics of the day and the ill-fated South Sea Company.

St Patrick's Cathedral

PATRICK STREET, DUBLIN, EIRE

Jonathan Swift was born at 7 Hoey's Court, Dublin, and educated at Kilkenny Grammar School, where one of his friends was William Congreve, the playwright. Swift then went to Trinity College (see above) and worked for the diplomat Sir William Temple (1628–99) after graduating.

Swift had strong Protestant convictions – he was ordained in Dublin in 1694 – but these clashed rather dramatically with his equally strong political beliefs. He spent a few years in England, but the heat generated by his politics sent him back to Dublin in 1714, where he took up the post of Dean of St Patrick's Cathedral, which had been offered to him the previous year. Swift continued to write inflammatory pamphlets, but from 1710 he was also engaged on *Journal to Stella*, which was a series of letters to a woman called Esther Johnson, and her companion, Rebecca Dingley. A great deal of uncertainty and speculation surrounds Swift's relationship with Esther, or 'Stella' as he called her. Was she his sister or niece, his lover, his friend or his wife? We do not know, but when Stella died in 1728 Swift was heartbroken, and after she was buried in the cathedral he spent his evenings here, completing his *Journal*.

Although Swift wrote a great many pamphlets and books, he is chiefly known for his satirical novel, *Gulliver's Travels* (1726). This was the only book for which he was paid – he received £200 for writing it. For most of his life Swift was troubled by what is now thought to have been Ménière's disease, which affected his balance, but the illness became more severe as he became older and in the end he was so ill that he was generally considered to be insane.

Swift died in 1745 and was buried in the nave of St Patrick's Cathedral, with his adored Stella beside him. Swift wrote his own epitaph in Latin, which was translated by W.B. Yeats. There is a bust of him on the wall of the south aisle. The cathedral also contains various items of Swift memorabilia, including the pulpit from where he used to preach.

After the death of Yeats in 1939, the Dean of St Patrick's suggested that the poet should be buried in the cathedral. He would have lain near Swift, who was an inspiration to him and about whom he wrote the play *The Words upon the Window-Pane* (1930). However, his family refused what would have been a great honour because Yeats had asked to be buried at Drumcliff Churchyard (see page 143) in his beloved Sligo.

ABOVE: The grim experience of living with an alcoholic father at 33 Synge Street turned George Bernard Shaw into a zealous teetotaller; he also abstained from meat, tea and coffee.

33 Synge Street

DUBLIN, EIRE

I am a typical Irishman: my family came from Yorkshire.' This was George Bernard Shaw's characteristically dry comment on his ancestry. He was born in Synge Street in July 1856, and was known to his family as 'Sonny'. Shaw spent the first ten years of his life in this house, the address of which was then 3 Upper Synge Street.

It was not a happy childhood, as his father was an alcoholic – which later prompted Shaw to become a strict teetotaller – whose wholesale grain business was slowly going broke. His mother was an heiress but was equally impoverished, and the combination was disastrous. Shaw and his siblings were mostly raised by the servants, but he bore his mother no ill will about her frequent absences.

The Shaw family moved to another part of Dublin in 1866, and young George went to the Wesley Connexional School (now Wesley College) on St Stephen's Green, followed by several other Dublin schools. However, Shaw's formal education ended at the age of 15, when he became a junior clerk at an estate agency in Molesworth Street. He later educated himself with the help of the British Museum's Reading Room.

In the meantime, Shaw's mother had decided to train as a singer and fallen in love with her singing teacher, George John Vandaleur Lee. When Lee went to London, Mrs Shaw and her daughter, Lucy, followed. In April 1876, Shaw left too, after a short stint working for a Dublin estate agent. He did not return to Ireland for another 30 years and even then he did not stay long. He certainly did not bother to come back for his father's funeral in 1885, and neither did his mother or his sisters.

Newman House

ST STEPHEN'S GREEN SOUTH, DUBLIN, EIRE

It sounds as though this is one house but actually it consists of two buildings: Nos 85 and 86, both of which are open to the public. The building was named after Cardinal John Henry Newman (1801–90), who was the first rector of the Catholic University of Ireland, which later became University College. The institution was founded in 1854 and offered Roman Catholic students the chance to attend a university in Dublin, because they were not allowed to take degrees at Trinity College Dublin (see pages 151–2).

James Joyce was one of the Catholic students who was able to study at the university, and he started there in 1898. Joyce knew Newman House as he once lectured to the 'L & H' (Literary and Historical Society) in the Physics Theatre, at the back of No. 85. Joyce also knew No. 86, because he studied in the classroom at the top floor of the house from 1899 to 1902.

The top floor of No. 86 also contains the bedroom that was occupied by the poet Gerard Manley Hopkins while he was Professor of Classics at the university from

ABOVE & BELOW: Newman House, a centre of learning and commemoration, has a fireplace dedicated to James Joyce (above) and a room in which Gerard Manley Hopkins spent the last years of his life feeling utterly dejected (below).

1884 to 1889. Hopkins was a Jesuit priest who was overwhelmed by his own sense of failure as a preacher. If he had hoped that teaching Greek and Latin in Dublin would be more satisfying than life as a parish priest he must have been bitterly disappointed. His period in Dublin was marked by depression and illness, as many of the 'Dark Sonnets' that he wrote during this time testify. Hopkins made a conscious effort to write work that was less bleak, but his gloom seems to have been a presentiment of trouble as he died from typhoid in 1889 at the age of 55. He was buried in the Jesuit plot in Glasnevin cemetery in Dublin. The playwright Brendan Behan (1923–64) is also buried in Glasnevin, as is Maud Gonne (1865–1953) who was the muse and unrequited love of W.B. Yeats.

Merrion Square

DUBLIN, EIRE

This is the grandest and most beautiful of the Georgian squares in the heart of Dublin. It seems to have acted like a magnet on some important literary figures since it was laid out in the 1770s, as the plaques on the buildings testify.

Joseph Sheridan Le Fanu (1814–73), who was born in Dominick Street, Dublin, and became one of the great masters of the ghost story, moved to 70 Merrion Square after the death of his wife in 1858. He became increasingly reclusive while he lived here, during which time he wrote several books, including his most chilling collection of tales, *In A Glass Darkly* (1872). The stories were published in three volumes, the final one containing a story called 'Carmilla' about a vampire with lesbian tendencies who had once belonged to the noble family of Karnstein in Styria.

'Carmilla' has often been cited as part of Bram Stoker's inspiration for *Dracula*, and sure enough the men knew each other. Stoker frequently visited the Wilde family, who were Le Fanu's neighbours at 1 Merrion Square, because he had been at Trinity College with their son, Oscar. Oscar's mother, Jane, enjoyed holding literary salons and Stoker enjoyed attending them. Stoker soon began to write theatrical reviews for the *Dublin Evening Mail*, of which Le Fanu was a part-owner. Some of the rooms at 1 Merrion

ABOVE: Insouciant even as a statue, Oscar Wilde graces Merrion Square where he once lived with his family. His mother, Jane, wrote poems under the name of Speranza.

Square are now open to the public, and there is a statue of Oscar Wilde, looking very relaxed, towards the north-west corner of the square.

The Wildes had long since left by the time that W.B. Yeats's wife, George, bought 82 Merrion Square at a knock-down price in 1922. Yeats did not approve of Wilde, believing that his excesses had not done literature any favours, so perhaps it is just as well that his family were no longer here. In 1923, Yeats was awarded the Nobel Prize for Literature. He first heard about it when Bertie Smyllie, the editor of *The Irish Times*, rang him at Merrion Square to break the news late one night. Yeats's immediate response was to ask 'How much, Smyllie, how much is it?' Yeats, George and their children, Anne and Michael, lived in the square until 1928 when they moved to a flat in Fitzwilliam Square, a few streets away.

Bibliography

Amis, Kingsley, *Memoirs*, Hutchinson, 1991

Bell, Quentin, *Virginia Woolf*, The Hogarth Press, 1972

Drabble, Margaret, and Stringer, Jenny, ed., *The Concise Oxford Companion to Literature*, OUP, 1990

Eagle, Dorothy and Carnell, Hilary, ed., *The Oxford Literary Guide to the British Isles*, OUP, 1977

Farson, Dan, *Soho in the Fifties*, Michael Joseph, 1987

Forster, Margaret, *Elizabeth Barrett Browning*, Chatto & Windus, 1988

Glendinning, Victoria, *Vita*, Weidenfeld & Nicolson, 1983

Greenwood, Margaret, Wallis, Geoff, Connolly, Mark and Hawkins, Hildi, *The Rough Guide to Ireland*, 7th edition, Rough Guides, 2003

Hardwick, Michael and Mollie, *The Charles Dickens Encyclopedia*, Futura, 1990

Hart-Davis, Rupert, ed., *Selected Letters of Oscar Wilde*, OUP, 1979

Hoare, Philip, *Noel Coward*, Sinclair-Stevenson, 1995

Humphreys, Rob, *The Rough Guide to London*, 5th edition, Rough Guides, 2003

Humphreys Rob and Reid, Donald, *The Rough Guide to Scotland*, 6th edition, Rough Guides, 2004

Humphreys Rob and Reid, Donald, *The Rough Guide to Scottish Highlands & Islands*, 3rd edition, Rough Guides, 2004

Jeffares, A. Norman, *W. B. Yeats*, Hutchinson, 1988

Karl, Frederick, *George Eliot*, HarperCollins, 1995

Lesley, Cole, *The Life of Noel Coward*, Jonathan Cape, 1976

Lesley, Cole, Payn, Graham and Morley, Sheridan, *Noel Coward and his Friends*, Weidenfeld & Nicolson, 1979

Lewis, Jeremy, *Cyril Connolly, A Life*, Jonathan Cape, 1997

Nicolson, Nigel, *Portrait of a Marriage*, Weidenfeld & Nicolson, 1973

O'Connor, Garry, *Sean O'Casey*, Hodder & Stoughton, 1988

Pearson, John, *Facades: Edith, Osbert and Sacheverell Sitwell*, Macmillan, 1978

Soames, Mary, *Clementine Churchill*, Cassell, 1979

Taylor, D. J., *Orwell, The Life*, Chatto & Windus, 2003

Varlow, Sally, *A Reader's Guide to Writer's Britain*, André Deutsch, 2004

Index

Acknowledgements

AUTHOR'S ACKNOWLEDGEMENTS

I have wanted to write a book like this for years, so it was a tremendous surprise and pleasure when Jo Hemmings at New Holland gave me this commission. I would like to thank her, my editor Kate Michell, and everyone else at New Holland who has worked so hard on this book. Thanks, too, to Chris Coe who has produced his usual collection of stunning photographs. And, as ever, most grateful thanks and love to those unsung heroes, Bill Martin and Chelsey Fox, without whom…

PICTURE ACKNOWLEDGEMENTS

Front cover (second top left) and page 33: National Portrait Gallery, London
Front cover (top right) and page 126: Mary Evans Picture Library/John Idris Jones
Page 52: LondonStills.com
Pages 78, 110, 136: Mary Evans Picture Library
Page 92: *The Tale of Benjamin Bunny* by Beatrix Potter, copyright © Frederick Warne & Co., 1904, 2002, reproduced by permission of Frederick Warne.
Page 98: Getty Images
Page 118: Mary Evans Picture Library/Thomas Gillmor Collection
Page 125: David Tipling